AF243932

Footprints in the Hills

*A collection of the life stories of some of Mudgee's
ten thousand residents*

in case of emergency press

We are proud to acknowledge the Traditional Owners of country throughout Australia and to recognise their continuing connection to land, waters, and culture.

We pay our respects to their Elders past, present, and emerging.

We support recognition, reconciliation, and reparation.

Footprints in the Hills

*A collection of the life stories of some of Mudgee's
ten thousand residents*

Mudgee Valley Writers

In Case Of Emergency Press

http://www.icoe.com.au
Travancore, Victoria
Australia

Published by In Case of Emergency Press 2019

Cover design: Narelle Noppert

ISBN 978-0-9943525-8-3

For my great great grandchildren. I would like them to look to the future. Look back to the past but don't dwell on it. Things change from minute to minute. Be happy in what you have got.

Steve Csuba

Table of contents

Introduction – Jill Baggett and Pamela Meredith

Jill Baggett

Pamela Meredith

Introduction

Recording the small pieces of the lives of Mudgee Elders has been a joy for me.

Such stories, such variety in the histories of these people now collected and held for coming generations to read and wonder.

Lives so different from today's young folks' experiences.

Pamela Meredith

As an initiative of Mudgee Valley Writers we have chosen just a few of our town's long time residents to share their life adventures, the happy times, great achievements and the difficult times.

The people in this book inspire me.

Jill Baggett.

Chapter 1 – Bob Campbell

Bob has had a life! His quote is 'An activist Folksinger' but there is so much more.

An ordinary person who has enjoyed an extraordinary life.

Bob Campbell

I was born in Maitland in February 1942, to parents Bob Campbell from Inverell and mother Catherine Ham from Sandy Hollow. My early life was dotted with violence and family breakup. My early schooling was at a convent in East Maitland, a Muswellbrook convent, the Giant's Creek public school at Sandy Hollow then a brief time at Muswellbrook High School before leaving home and school at fourteen.

My father was a painter and docker, a jack-of-all-trades, a footballer, and a boxer. His nickname "The Bull" tells his story. An early memory is of my mother putting my little brother and me in a pram and going to pick gum tips at Fairy Dell alongside the road to Newcastle. Red gum tips were placed in vases in the house as flowers. Our life on the outskirts of East Maitland next to the shanty town of corrugated iron huts, from the time of the depression was straight out of Henry Lawson's The Drover's Wife. Fairy Dell is now the Green Hills Shopping Centre.

I have worked at many occupations, brick maker, bush labourer, apprentice plasterer and hotel worker in many parts of the world. After marrying at seventeen I worked on the Townsville to Mt Isa railway. I had a couple of years at BHP in Newcastle and then to Wormald's factory. This is where my involvement in trade unions began. I eventually spent ten years as a full-time union organizer for the AMWSU, an amalgamation between the Sheet Metal Workers, the Engineering Union and the Boilermakers union.

During my time with the unions I attended University at night to attain a BA degree and teacher training. German language was part of my degree. Music has carried me around the world. As well as busking in England I have worked as a pizza cook, worked in an Irish pub and played music full time in Germany.

After finishing my Diploma of Education and working with the late Dr Sharon Frost on a cattle property outside Coolah, I accepted an appointment to teach English and History at Gulgong High School before establishing a German Language department at the school. I eventually received scholarships to study in Germany and moved to Berlin playing music and working with the Foreign Affairs Department promoting Australia alongside aboriginal groups, artists and wine makers in 1992. I continued working as a musician in Berlin until 1997 when I returned to Australia and took up a position at Red Hill Environmental Education Centre where I worked for more than ten years before retiring as Principal in 2011. During all this time I continued playing music with my band Home Rule and as a solo artist. My maternal Grandmother was an Irish fiddler. My Catholic education and Irish background established a lifelong passion for Irish fiddle music, folk songs and poetry. Over the past thirty-five years I have made many CD's most with Sharon Frost. I am attracted to words, have always remembered words of poems and songs from childhood.

My life as a political and social activist stems from a hatred of injustice and unfairness. I have long been interested in politics, opposing the Vietnam War and joining the Australian Communist Party, as they were the only party protesting the war and, as I saw it then, working for a better world. I believe there is much injustice in the world and the powerful will always exploit the weak wherever possible and I encourage the weak to stand up for themselves, each other and for our planet.

I have no interest in sport despite my father being one of ten children who were involved in boxing and rugby league at the highest levels. The women of the family didn't play sport and it was from the women that I developed a love of poetry and music. I feel fortunate that there has always been someone to encourage me along the way despite my impoverished background. My younger brother and I were in an orphanage for a while and at fifteen, I spent seven months in a boy's home. Someone always gave me a leg up through my young life.

I believe I have accumulated a lot of wisdom from philosophers and poets such as Shakespeare and Goethe, men of literature. I have been a great reader of novels but now read mainly poetry and the daily newspapers and magazines. I believe we need to understand the Greek philosophers and the great literature including the bible to know more about human behaviour and emotion. This should result in respect for other humans and teach us not to do harm to anyone or our fragile planet.

I believe the most pressing single issue in Australia is to understand Aboriginal peoples, their culture and rights. My seven and 4-year-old step grandchildren are Wiradjuri. Recently I went to Newcastle for NAIDOC week celebrations with them and their grandmother. I always included and taught aboriginal education at Gulgong High School and Red Hill. I have studied aboriginal politics, land rights and culture and sang at the first Aboriginal Embassy in Canberra. I have written and performed songs on local aboriginal history and have a song about the legendary Pemulwuy included on two ABC Compilation Albums. I have written and presented a radio program on Jimmy Governor.

The person I most admire in politics is Bob Brown; he walked away from a corporate career. Also Ted Mack, he retired the day before he qualified for a Parliamentary Pension. There is a place for Independents in our government. Most politicians move to working for big corporations these days when they retire from government. When I was a union organizer, after the amalgamation, I stepped down after two terms in accordance with communist party policy. I think this would be a good idea for current politicians although there are some honest ones. Democracy is shaky at the moment with so many dictators around. To rubbish all politicians is to risk going back to dictatorships. The example of Hitler's Germany is something to keep in mind. When a section of the community is portrayed as less than human, cruelty and lack of compassion can be justified by leaders as is currently happening with refugees.

The battlers have realized they have to stand up for themselves and vote.

I quote Gandhi: "Become the change you want to see." My book 'Giants Leap' is the story of my life as an activist, folk singer and writer of songs.

Chapter 2 – Thelma Winter

A life so full.

Years of operating the local Windeyer post office and manual telephone exchange. Thelma shares the most joyful laughter with family and friends.

Thelma Winter

I was born at Hillview property between Windeyer and Pyramul. My parents were Cecil Hawkins and Mary Whittaker. Dad was bought up at Grattai, mother and her nine sisters were bought up at Collingwood.

I am the middle child of three girls, Ina and Reta my sisters. A stillborn baby was born first and there is a memorial for her at Collingwood—an area on the way to Mudgee from Windeyer.

My first memory is of going around the sheep with my parents, sometimes on horseback when we lived at Hillview, we walked to check the ewes with lambs.

Dad always took us away on holidays. Often fishing at Walgett and Bourke in the rivers. We children sat in the back of the truck and hung on at a time when the roads were all gravel. We also went to the coast and to the wool sales in Sydney when he would take extra days and take us to Manly on the ferry. Special times.

I went to Windeyer School from 1945 until 1952, it had two classrooms and went from kindergarten to year 6 when I attended. Many local children only went to school until the end of primary school. I rode a pushbike there and back each day. We boarded at Phillip's near the river for two years. I loved school and was never in the punishment book. I was Captain with Barry Wilson in Year 6.

I came to work here at the post office when I left school, employed by the Hooper's. I lived with them at the post office house and became like a daughter to them. The original house had burnt down and the current one had been built by voluntary local labour in 1929. It was a much better building. Bertha Wells was the occupant then when I was going to school.

When I first worked at the post office it was the telephone exchange, general store and Commonwealth Bank agency. It was called the GPO in those days.

Years later when it changed to Telecom and Australia Post it was never the same. Party lines were fun when one party wouldn't get off the line. Operating hours were 8 AM till 6 PM and then it changed to 7 AM to 9 PM and 7 AM till midday on Saturdays. On weekends there was an opening fee of 30 cents for out of hours calls. Other exchanges were at Pyramul, Sally's Flat,

Hargraves, Meroo and Hill End. My daughter Della worked at some of these exchanges too.

1984 the telephone exchange was shut down. 1985 the post office closed.

Nowadays Australia Post is at the Windeyer Caravan Park. We have mail deliveries from Mudgee five days a week, but they won't bring bread or special parcels like they used too.

Our social life included dances at Hargraves, Grattai, Windeyer, Pyramul and Sally's Flat. Dad had a car and so did my husband Barry's father. In those days you could watch the cars go past and know who was going by to town.

When there was a fire in the area I knew where everyone was, and I organised the sandwiches and drinks. I had no sleep on nights when there was a fire locally. Now it is organised by the Rural Fire Brigade.

My husband Barrington James Winter and I had three children—Susan Mary born in 1960, Vincent Cecil born 1961 and Della May born 1962. Barry passed away in 1995, our son Vincent in 1984. My children all went to Windeyer School.

I have had constant connection to the Windeyer School, working as a Teacher's Aide with craft and cooking and volunteering in many ways—coaching tennis, athletics and swimming. I attended many Small School Sports Days.

The Director General of Education gave me an award for long service to the Windeyer School.

After Barry died, I enjoyed my friendship with Ross Lovett and had a beautiful life travelling with him. There was hardly a spot in New South Wales we didn't visit as he travelled for work.

If I die tonight, I have had a beautiful life.

Chapter 3 – James Percy Thompson

Percy Thompson—from childhood hardship to Mayor of Mid-Western Regional Council. A man of many talents. Over many years he has given his time and efforts to our community.

A family man.

James Percy Thompson

A Valentine's birth date 14th February 1944 at Eugowra, along the Lachlan River. My parents were Elva Mary Rawsthorne from Forbes and Percy Alan Thompson from Cowra. My father was one of 14 children.

We had no electricity until I was fifteen.

I began kindergarten at Eugowra. We moved to live at Cooyal between the White and Red Munghorn—there is still a big pepper tree where the house stood, now in the National Park. I walked 10 kilometres to school and then ten back when we lived at Wollar. Then Stubbo, where we lived in a tent and I used to sleep in the back of a Land Rover. We used to be tormented over having no house.

One of the bus drivers drove an International truck and we kids sat along the sides of the tray, he had a bad stutter and would say, '—Iffff you Thompsons keep fightttttiinnngg I'll put ppppuuuutt you off." He never did.

When Dad had enough money, he bought forty-five acres outside Gulgong where we had an old house with a big verandah, my four sisters slept at one end and I slept on the back verandah. I used to get wheat bags from the shed for warmth in the winter.

At Gulgong Red Hill School, I'd be sat at the front for talking. Teacher didn't like me and threw a blackboard duster at me; I threw it back and hit him between the eyes. My sister was two classes ahead of me and the teacher didn't like her either. He used to call her 'little black mongrel.' We have Indian blood on father and mothers' sides. That teacher used to cane me every day. I still have damaged fingers.

One day he went out of the room and came back and asked everyone, "Who was talking?" He accused me but I hadn't been talking and wouldn't hold out my hand to be caned. "Put it out, put your hand out." "No, I won't." He bent over me to hit my backside and I punched him in the stomach. Other teachers came and took me to the Headmaster, but he took my side. I wouldn't apologise so was kept back after school. My mother came, but I still wouldn't apologise, and he never caned me again, but he called me a black mongrel and wouldn't put my sister in the top class. After school each day I had to chop wood, milk cows and feed pigs. I should have punched that teacher eighteen months earlier and spared me so much pain from canings.

I got on well with the headmaster and he told me I had the highest IQ of the children he had taught in thirty-three years and told me I could be a doctor, barrister or scientist. I got my Intermediate Certificate at the Gulgong school.

When I was sixteen, I caught 19 wild horses near Cook's Gap. There were only two houses there then. I roped the stallion and took him to the yards. He started whinnying and the other horses all came running into the yards to him. I called the stallion Lucky, broke the others in and sold them, but Lucky, I gelded him, and he became real quiet and lots of people learnt to ride on him.

I was the Junior Champion Sportsperson in Gulgong. I won the under 16 Championship of Mudgee District when I was 15 and beat the State Champion by five yards although I was running barefoot. This was at Victoria Oval in Mudgee.

I played first grade football for Gulgong on the wing at 16 then for Dunedoo and Wellington.

I played cricket and opened the batting for the school for three years.

My mother bought a pony called Star Spangled Banner and I won Champion Rider at Zone 6 Pony Club. I also won The Flag and Bending Race. In one of the Flag and Bending races I won by miles and went around behind the judges, the second place getter was given the 1st prize, a woman spoke up and said, "You are wrong this young fellow came 1st," but the judge said, "Judges' decision is final." I won lots of prizes in shows around. I rode my horse through 'The Burr Paddock' to school, there were mines through there too. It is now the golf course.

I got up at 4 AM to milk six cows and feed fifty pigs. Then would ride to the racecourse and do trackwork. I was a good buckjump rider. Bruce Parkinson bred a horse called Paw Paw. Nobody could ride it, when he threw you, he'd try to paw you. We were staying in the shearing huts and I said I'd have a go at riding the horse, they said he'd kill me. I rode him then on cut out day and he had three goes at throwing me, but he could not. Bruce arrived in a Humber Super Snipe at our house that night and offered to take me for a milkshake and said I could have the horse, but my mother said NO.

No one else could ride him. Fine Cotton was also bred at Ben Buckley.

My Great Grandfather Maurice Rawsthorne took a horse from Forbes to run in the Melbourne Cup. It won the race before the Cup, Socan Cup. It was a flag start.

My Great Grandfather was an engineer on the railway between Lithgow and Gulgong and then Bathurst and Cowra. His family name from England was Treasure. While he was in Gulgong an Indian lady had a café and her daughter was a half caste and he married her. There were 20,000 people in Gulgong digging for gold, 11 hotels at Two Mile Flat and 56 hotels in Gulgong. My great grandmother on my mother's side was a Scot but had Indian blood. Great grandfather had land from Canowindra to Cowrawabbity, now a Federal Heritage House.

They had a Queen Competition at Gulgong to raise money for a swimming pool. I had broken an ankle when a horse hit a post with me but still won the buck jumping and bull ride. When my mother found out she went mad at Bill Gudgeon and wouldn't let me have the trophies. Nearly fifty years later Mrs. Alexander gave me those trophies.

I also played polo cross, was a jockey and rode a few winners.

I was an amateur boxer, had my first fight at 14. There was a boxing tournament at the Gulgong Hall, my school teacher told me to enter and I got the Fighter of the Night. I was wearing gloves for the first time. My father had told me I could enter but not to tell my mother. But then it ended up in the Gulgong paper!

My first job was droving cattle for Jack Gilham and then roustabouting with Hilton Bennett, who won the shearing competition in front of the Queen in 1954. At sixteen I learnt wool classing at Tech and got a job three days shearing, and I remember the back ache. I then had a Holden ute. I shore 100 sheep a day, then after six months it was 200 and after twelve months it was 300. I decided to be a full-time shearer. I played football at the same time as a paid player.

The Contractor at Haddon Rig talked me into shearing in a competition. I was very nervous the first time but went on to win forty-seven Open Championships and at times beat the best shearers in the world.

I married Diane Mary Griffiths when I was eighteen. I had to borrow money from her to buy the ring. I was roustabouting at the time and one night before cutout we went to Goolma Pub. I had my first beer there and started singing. Diane came in and listened to me singing. Her father said I was a 'no hoper'.

We married in Bathurst and went to her grandparents' place afterwards for a party. I was still working for my father and received little wages. We lived with my parents for a while then rented from a Gulgong lady for three pounds a week. I then share farmed with my father but didn't get a good crop. My son James Percy Junior was born and the lady who we rented from said not to bother paying her rent as we had a baby to care for. The house had no electricity and a fuel stove, a chip heater and we poked newspaper in the holes in the walls to block the wind.

We had five children and when our eldest son went to school, we got a Housing Commission Home in Madeira Road Mudgee. We wanted to buy it then my father in law died and I arranged the lease to be given to my mother in law.

We took over the hotel in Goolma, promised a five-year lease if we could get the kegs sold up to 5 kegs a week. We built it up to 12x18 gallon kegs a week and then leased it. I was still shearing and contracting, and Diane and a cousin ran the hotel while I was away. I took thirty-six dozen bottles to the shed to sell to the shearers. I had my first shearing contract outside Gulgong. Then when they had the big sheep numbers I had 1,000,000 sheep a year contracts from Cunnamulla to Queanbeyan. I had two to three teams and also did two nights a week working at the pub when home. We shore 45,000 sheep on one property outside Queanbeyan. We started the Rugby Union Club and played competitions in the Central Districts the following year, we won the comp in Orange. We also started a Pony Club at Goolma.

We bought the Freehold of the hotel then I leased it and bought 45 acres in Gulgong; it had been my father's property. I then bought a bigger farm at Mebul, called it Mornington after my grandfather's place at Cowra. I was still running shearing teams and the bank manager in Gulgong cut my bank overdraft. Wool prices fell in the early 1990's too. I had to sell the hotel and I changed my bank then.

I borrowed from the Rural Bank and bought the first Open Front Header that came to the district. I used to drive it day and night when I wasn't shearing, contracting or wheat carting, that I did in a Diamond T truck. A Common Knocker, very strong trucks.

I was a successful horse trainer. I trained winners on twenty-six different tracks. I bred and trained Star of Universe and he was NSW Country Horse of the Year in the 2005/6 season and won 26 races altogether.

We originally had 1200 acres at Mebul and have 700 acres left, the best country. Our grandson rents the place now and we live in the house. He recently sold 400 merino ewes for $220 each!

I write poems and sing songs. I was lead singer in the choir at school and went on to sing on radio and in clubs.

In 1987 I was elected onto Mudgee Council. After a few years I was Deputy Mayor and then elected Mayor.

I had six terms as Mayor and have been on Council for thirty-two years.

Our family is now five children, 22 grandchildren and 7 great grandchildren.

Chapter 4 – Cora Passer

Cora is a woman of many talents. Her life story is so interesting.

Cora Passer

To begin I was born in 1933 of Dutch parents living in Sumatra. My arrival a surprise for my family.

School days were in the mountains where my brother and sister travelled with me in a bus that broke down often and provided us with time to explore the countryside. Our school lessons were in Dutch.

The first experience of the war was the bombing by the Japanese of the harbour in the distance. Families were rounded up and walked to buses carrying whatever they could. For a time, they were held in a school then taken by train to a prison camp in Bangkimang, which was our home for four years.

Women and children were in one camp and men in another. My brother was moved to the men's huts when he turned 12. Men were allowed out of the compound to hunt for food and herbs and to gather wood. I saw my father working in the prison garden and didn't recognise him as he had a long beard and a moustache, and I said, "That's not my Pappy."

Our life in the camp was tolerable. No cruelty but not enough food. We caught rats and mice for the sick in the hospital (not a happy memory.) When we were able to go out around the camp and gather herbs and plants to eat, we had secret pockets to hide away pieces just for us. My mother, my sister and I lived on the second level of the hut.

The woman boss in charge was a Dutch/Indonesian who was good enough to us.

We washed in a hut with a long channel running through it and we used a dipper to fill and pour over us. One naughty young fellow swam the length of the channel and ducked up in the section that was divided off for the nuns. Other sections were for women and children.

My father was released to work in the cement works, he arranged for us to stay at the factory accommodation with him. Some of the Japanese guards would have tea with us. They missed their family. Bags of cement were shipped from the wharves to Japan. Americans bombed these ships transporting cement.

I was 13 when the day of liberation came, a beautiful big red sunrise I remember. Indian and British soldiers parachuted in to rescue us.

The Indonesians wanted to kill us, the Dutch, so we waited at the camp to be taken to another camp run by the allies. From there I used to sneak out to go roller-skating.

I remember when I met my first husband at a swimming pool. I saw him walk by in a white suit and thought he looked arrogant. I married him 3 months later. He aged 30 and I was 17. I had my first child when I was 18, together we had 4 children, all born in Indonesia.

There were more upheavals after the war when there were clashes between Java and Sumatra. Friends came to our house and told us to escape. Rebels were bombing villages. Our family drove from Padang, but roads were washed out and we hid in the Lake Toba area, another frightening time.

Malaysia was a stopover in safety where we went to the embassies applying for emigration to USA, Canada, New Zealand and Australia.

My husband was part Indonesian and his mother often dressed in a sarong. There was a White Australian Policy in those years, but he did manage to pass as 'white'.

A military ship took us from Malaysia to Singapore. It had no side railings and sharks cruised around.

In the early 1980's we were told we could go to Australia by boat, but my parents had money hidden in their clothes, so they bought plane tickets.

We settled in Australia happily.

My first husband died in 1986. I married again in 1989.

My son is an important part of my life now. Children come to Mudgee for visits in the summer time.

My eldest son was killed in a car accident. Several months ago, he came to me in a dream saying

'Don't worry Mam, you will be alright.'

It was so real I looked around for him when I awoke.

My life in Australia has been happy and in my later years I have had interests in many crafts. Bobbin lace and tatting are favourites and I have taught these crafts with U3A at the Adams Street rooms.

Spinning and knitting and crochet fill many of my days. My home has many examples of my works.

Chapter 5 – Istvan "Steve" Peter Csuba

Steve is a man who has lived a life of adventure. Smiles and warmth greet friends always.

Steve Csuba

Steve is my name. I was born in January 1933 in Hungary.

My parents Jozsef Csuba and Elias Maria were both born in Hungary.

I have an early memory of walking with my mother holding my hand and an old lady saying what a nice smile I had.

We lived in a village, Topolca which is about the size of Mudgee, a rural town in the St. George Basin—there are hills around like Mudgee and a river to swim in like the Cudgegong.

I was very shy when I attended kindergarten, there was a rocking horse I wanted to ride but I was too shy.

At six I went to the local school for four years, I hated school by the way. High School for only one year, failing in Hungarian and maths. My mother made me study during the holidays, but I failed again in second year. We were very poor, and mother paid the tutor with a chicken. Note: There are 48 letters in the Hungarian alphabet.

My father died in 1944 when I was eleven. Schooling went on until Year Eleven and I came second because I wanted to do it. An apprenticeship to go to after school with a cabinet maker who was very wise, and I learnt a lot from him. The communists took over when I was fourteen, I thought communism was stupid, I had read a lot. When I was fifteen, I planned to escape from Hungary. I didn't tell anyone I was leaving.

My boss and a friend introduced me to a group to run away with. The leader of the group was nineteen and I sixteen. I had sold some of my father's tools to buy cigarettes. We escaped to a border town, it was February 1949 and there was still snow on the ground. We were led to a railway station to Austria, in the Russian Section. The country was divided into different sections. American, English, French and Russian zones.

We were in the Russian zone and were caught by the Russian guards and were taken to a guard house and interviewed and charged with smuggling, all four of us. When one of the other boys were being interviewed, we pinched back the cigarettes that had been taken from us. The Russians were going to take us back to Hungary but when the border guards left only one man to guard us, we decided to make a run for it. We ran four different ways, two ran into the forest and I don't know what happened to them, Louis didn't run. I ran and heard, "Stop or I'll shoot!" He didn't shoot me but belted me with the rifle butt. Luckily, I was wearing two sets of clothes, Sunday best underneath and working clothes on top. He took me back to the guard house and made me stand in the corner. He patted Louis on the back and told him he was a good boy for not running and then gave him the food I had brought. I was very cranky with that.

A nice-looking girl came in and asked why we were running away. I said I wanted to go to America to make my fortune. The guard then said, "Go back to Hungary," so we ran back to the forest. The guards shot at us as we ran. The snow was about two inches deep and it was very eerie. I was tired and I heard sounds like someone stalking us, but it was birds finding their nests. We ate snow leaning against trees as it was too cold to lay down, we stamped our feet to stop them freezing. All night we heard trains, and then roosters crowing at dawn. We didn't know where we were. We knew we needed to go west and went by the sun. I now seemed to be the leader.

There was a farmhouse on the edge of the forest, we wanted food. As we waited till dark, we could hear people talking, then two Austrian policemen walked past. I said to Louis, 'I'm going to the farmhouse and if you see me running you run for your life.' The Austrian lady at the farmhouse was very nice and she gave me bread and lard, pork fat, and some for my friend too. I told her I wanted to go to the American section, she told me to walk to the village where there was an old Hungarian man. 'Watch out for police on patrol.'

I found the house, a young man came to the gate of the house and I asked if anyone spoke Hungarian, he introduced me to his grandfather. "I don't like the communists and am escaping to America". He gave us food and told me of a lady who lived on the outskirts of the next village who would help. I found the lady and she spoke Hungarian. She said, 'Be careful, the next village is on the border of the English zone, go to the pub, there is a lady there who also speaks Hungarian.'

When we told her where we had come from, she said her son was in my home town buying wine for the pub. 'Wait until dark and go to the river, there is a guard house.' We went. I took off my boots there was still snow on the ground. The river was like the Cudgegong, I sank to my neck. Cigarettes and all wet. Crossing wasn't hard but I couldn't climb the bank on the other side. I kept saying to Louis to come but he was too scared. There was an Alsatian dog up on the bank. I struggled up and took my clothes off and wrung them out while they started to freeze solid.

Knocking on six or seven doors of homes they all chased me away. I finished up at the village centre at the well. I saw a light burning in a window and a lady and daughter stirring jam. I started knocking on the window and saying, 'I want to sleep.' She covered the window with a blanket. A man came and talked at a million to one and I found out he was scared of me. I was scared of him. I followed him to a big farmhouse, he used a big castle key to unlock the gate, then used a smaller key to unlock a door and took me into a kitchen with a stove burning. I took a wet cigarette out of my pocket and offered it to him, he took it and dried it on the stove. This made him happy. He had four oxen and milking cows in a stable. He started to clean the cows with a brush, I found another brush and started to help, he was thrilled I was helping.

By morning I was almost dry. Two men came in and they were speaking in Austrian/German, different to High German. One of them, a big tall man, said, 'Come.' He took me to the outside of the village, introduced me to his wife. They gave me a room, bath, buttons for my clothes which were in a bad state, fed me, and showed me how to milk a cow. They owned land across the river as well in the other zone.

I was there for about a month and had started to pick up the language. I told the farmer I needed papers if I was going to stay. They adopted me as their son. One morning he said we would go to the city to the British Commander. We hopped on a bus and he took me to the office.

There was a big man, a Slav, who was a translator, he spoke Hungarian and English and he told them my story. The highlight for me was they bought breakfast. Coffee, white bread and English marmalade. I thought I was in heaven. I remember the white bread spread with butter and marmalade.

I was told, 'don't speak to anyone,' and was put in a cell but he didn't lock the door, gave me a piece of paper and I went to the pub and had a beautiful meal.

I remember another Hungarian with a trench coat and a limp, he looked like a spy, they locked him up. I don't know what happened to him. But nothing nice.

Next morning, I was given money and taken to the city and locked up in a jail, giving food from the pub again. I spent one night there and then an English army truck came and took me and other men many miles to a camp surrounded by barbwire. We discovered that it was called Straw Camp. There were hundreds, mostly Hungarians, sleeping only on straw with no bedclothes for a few weeks. I learnt to eat food with no utensils. I found a 400-gram tin and I would fill it up with food that was very hot, eat it quickly, and then I'd line up again in the queue for more. I was sixteen at the time. All men in the camp and we played soccer.

One day the guard told me someone was looking for me at the gate. It was the farmer and he gave me food and drink, which I shared, but when the others got something from the Red Cross they didn't share.

We were taken to another camp run by the British Secret Service where we were interrogated individually. You couldn't leave till you got a job. Every Thursday they had a 'slave market.' You would strip to your waist and farmers would come and check you over, muscles and teeth just like a slave market. You could only leave if a farmer took you. A lady came and chose me, but my Guardian Angel told me not to go. The lady gave me instructions and signed the papers, I said I would come to her place the next day as I had things to collect. I walked out the gate and went the other way from her farm. I didn't want to go with her.

Another pub in another village, the publican told me to wait in his room and he would bring me something to eat. Two or three hours later he came and said he had found me a job. There was a farmer, he gave me 10 shillings and full board, my own room. He had four cows, two calves, four oxen and it was my job to feed and look after them and to harness them up ready for work. I was there for nearly a year.

His daughter, Erika, a university student, was on holidays, she was engaged to an architect. My job was to heat the water in a big barrel for everyone to have a bath. One day I made up the bath and there is the farmer's wife, a massive big lady standing up, she started screaming but I was too frightened to move. I saw my first naked lady. I kept saying, "I'm sorry, I'm sorry."

When the daughter was home, I was last to have a bath. As the daughter came past, she grabbed me and kissed me. I thought she was going to eat me with her French kissing. Then I decided I liked it and thought I was in love. And I got ten-shilling bonus.

Later a bloke came up and was kissing her outside my window and I was so jealous I was going to kill him. I had a 22 rifle I used to shoot apples out of the tree. I didn't know which of them to shoot first. I felt a big slap and one of the soldiers took the gun and told me she'd just been having fun with me. I tried to join the Foreign Legion, but I was too young.

I went to the International Refugee Organisation, they showed me a map and asked me where I wanted to go. I saw a big island, Australia. They took me to Salzburg, and I had a medical examination and I waited in a hostel for a few months. We had a house mother there who used to give us castor oil and lollies.

I finally arrived in Australia in 1950. They took us by train to Germany and then by ship to Fremantle. The camps there were worse than the ones in Europe. I had never heard English and privacy was a rope and a blanket. We were brought here because Australia didn't have enough workers. You had to work for two years where you were placed by Australian Immigration.

After a couple of weeks, a man came from Perth and gave me a job mixing concrete for roofing tiles. Perth people were beautiful, Western Australia was rural, friendly and you could leave a bag on the street and days later it would still be there. I did concreting for about a year till my English improved. I earned three pounds a week, cheap labour. One day the boss said if I made 50 more tiles a day, he would pay me more. I said we won't have smoko or long lunch and we made 750 tiles a day, but the bugger wouldn't pay us. One day I folded my arms and said, 'Nothing happening,' to the foreman. When the boss came, I said I wasn't going to work anymore. He picked up a shovel, but I had an iron bar. He rang the Perth office and said I was a troublemaker. The bloke in the office was very nasty to me. I said, 'I want a transfer to Midland Junction Office,' in a different jurisdiction. I went by train and said what had happened, the officer said to go and ask for a dry cleaner presser's job. I got the job and worked for Jeff for five years. He gave me an extra ten shillings a week.

I was getting adult wages at seventeen. He had two dry cleaning businesses. I was the Foreman.

This was the beginning of the good life for me.

Every Thursday I knocked off early and rowed for the WA Rowing Club. After a while the boss came to me and told me that everyone knocked off early after I left on Thursdays. So, I didn't leave early after that.

One of my friends said I'd earn a lot of money if I went to work at Maralinga. Seventeen dollars a week. I went to their office and said I'd work as a labourer.

We were building facilities for the Atomic Centre. It was hard work and I thought I'd apply for an easier job as a Diesel Engineer's assistant. I said I could drive a tractor. The foreman asked, "What can you do?"—"Nothing—but show me and I will be able to do it." I did grinding wells. I am a visual learner.

Later

In 1974 I had just opened a dry-cleaning business in Mudgee when I had a feeling I had to go—Mum wanted to see me. I packed up and left in a week. Mum had been in bed for 12 months, dying, waiting for me to come home. She got up next day after I arrived. I went to see my brother in Budapest and there was a telegram. Mum had passed away.

Another time I felt I had to ring home. It cost $75 to ring. I rang at 7 AM but it took nearly a full day to get through. My brother went to the post office to take the call. My mother was in hospital and I could talk to her.

A memory to hold forever—my mother is my Guardian Angel. And when I met Eils, my wife of 35 years.

For my great great grandchildren. I would like them to look to the future. Look back to the past but don't dwell on it. Things change from minute to minute. Be happy in what you have got.

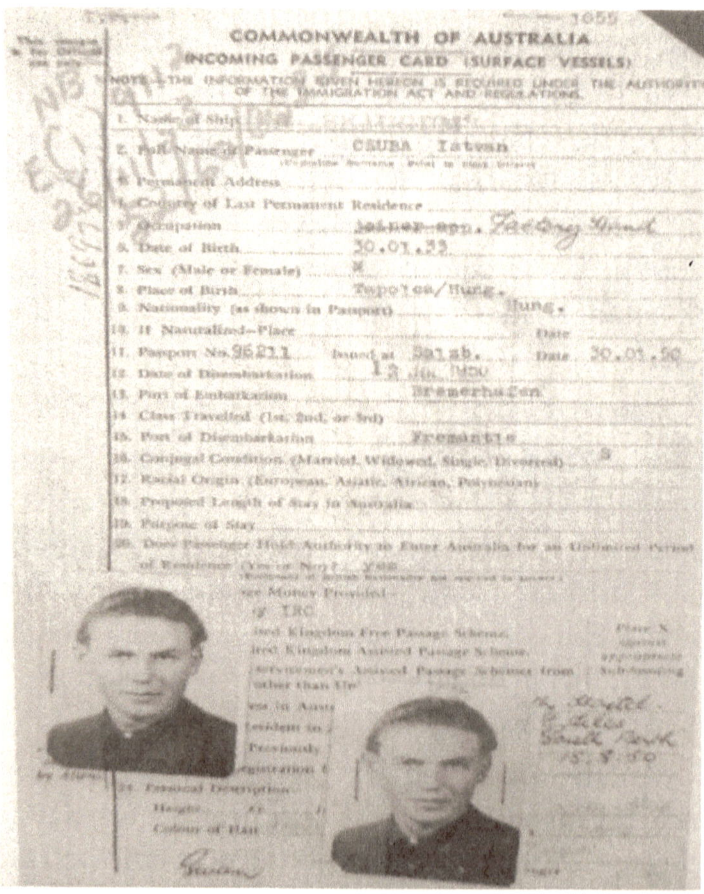

Chapter 6 – Annemary Denley

Annie to her friends. A woman of action, community minded.

This year 2019 Annie is Mudgee's Senior Person of the Year. Well deserved.

Annie Denley

I was born in September 1945. My parents were Stella McMullen and John Sneddon. He left his wife and three children the day I was born. My mother told me he noticed the bruise on my forehead and said, "Stella, the sins of the father are born forth on the child," and with that he left. I didn't meet my father again until I was 20 years old.

Memories that I hold of my childhood are strong. I went to Merewether pre-school. My mother decided to go to a Brewarrina sheep station called Uri Point as a housekeeper. Then it became time for me to go to school.

My Earliest Memory is from when I was four and a half when I watched my mother walk away from that convent in Brewarrina. I was watching from the window and have scars still from chewing at the louvers on the window as she left. An everyday memory for me. She had told me I was going to a party, then she just left me. I lived with the nuns till I was eleven years old. This is when I had a nervous breakdown and had to leave the convent. It was a fitting end to a terrible experience.

My mother came to the convent. We went to Newcastle and stayed with relatives while I got treatment and recovered quite quickly.

From the age of twelve I worked on a sheep station at Cunnamulla as a house maid. The nuns had found me the job and my mother went back to work.

My schooling wasn't good, and I had some education through Blackfriars Correspondence School.

My brother worked on a property close to me at Cunnamulla and had a ute. He came to get me, and we went to Sydney and stayed at The People's Palace.

I attended TAFE for a year to learn hairdressing, qualifying as a third-year apprentice.

I obtained work at Peter Austin Salon in the St. James Building in Sydney for two years after which I obtained my license. I lived in a hostel at Darling Point. Ladies who came to the salon were upmarket women and tipped when you took their furs. I loved the job but contracted chemical poisoning and had to stop. After that I taught hairdressing at Hornsby TAFE and then I obtained a Barber's License.

My working life has been varied.

I managed property with my de facto husband, and we owned a food catering van.

After separation at Kilcoy I moved to Mudgee.

I cleaned houses, including Havilah in Mudgee.

These days I volunteer with Blaze Aid fencing and cooking. For seventeen years I have been a Community Driver, including time in Queensland. I love driving.

As well as sketching, painting, bird watching, long walks and gardening around my lovely apartment.

My most vivid memory is my eldest child being born in Hornsby Hospital after a three-day labour, I was 28 years old.

Most important person in my life was my first husband Brian.

I met a wise black man at Goodooga, Shilling Jackson, an Aboriginal Elder, his mother was named Queen Mary and his son Sixpence. He told wonderful stories. One was how to know when emus were laying eggs.

I am honest, compassionate and can be asked to do any job. Water is my drink of choice.

For my Great Grandchildren: Whoever you are I love you now. Love is all there is and it's free. Never tell lies, always the truth.

Chapter 7 – Joy Hibberd

Joy Mary Hibberd's life has been eventful. She loves her family and follows her hobbies with passion.

Joy Hibberd

I was born in November 1938 in Salisbury England. My birth mother was Violet Baker and my adopting parents Ernest and Beatrice Hibberd.

My first memory is when I was perhaps 3 or 4, it was raining and cold, living in Salisbury. My dad came and got me out of bed to show me a big glow in the sky—it was the blitz bombing of Southampton, 30 kilometres from Salisbury.

We had an air raid shelter in the garden but didn't experience much bombing but there was a siren which used different sounds for 'warnings' and 'all safe'. They also used barrage balloons to warn people, we could see them lifted into the air as deterrents to planes coming to bomb.

There were two boys, evacuees living with us for about three years, from when they were 10 to 13 years old. One was from a well to do family and did have some contact with his parents, the other from a family of thirteen in Liverpool and he had little contact with his family.

I started school at All Saints in Harnham then in high school went to St Edmunds. They were Church of England schools.

I wasn't so much 'put down' by my mother, I was compared to my adopted older cousins a lot. When I was ten, I found out I was adopted in an unfortunate way—someone in our street told me.

I myself wanted to go to South Wilts Grammar in Salisbury, but the recent upsets that had occurred when I discovered I was adopted caused me to stop concentrating. I failed the exam. So my mother wanted me to go to boarding school in Trowbridge. I didn't want to, so I purposely failed that exam.

I went to St Edmunds, a public school for four years. My parents weren't unkind to me, they were rather toffee nosed. I was nothing like them. They used to dress me in posh, frilly clothes but I rebelled against this once I got to about seven. I liked it out of town, riding my bicycle and climbing trees. I used to wander alone through the fields and woods.

There is one fun story that I love to tell.

I belonged to the Junior Red Cross and wore the uniform—was a white skirt and navy shirt. Our group travelled to Trowbridge for a big occasion, we were to be presented to Princess Margaret. I was sat in the front row as I was the best dressed, my mother was very posh. As I was sitting Princess Margaret came along, she was very young, and stopped in front of me. I knew I was supposed to get up and curtsy but there was no room, so I stayed seated. A big fat Red Cross woman came and pulled me to my feet, almost knocking the Princess over, I was so embarrassed. Princess Margaret whispered to me, 'Don't worry.'

That fat woman told the leader from Salisbury. More embarrassment. I was about thirteen and I will never forget meeting Princess Margaret.

On the whole I had a happy childhood. Dad and I went for walks on the downs and meadows, even in the snow. I loved those walks together in all weathers.

After school my first job was in a hardware store, then I went to Debenhams department store, a bit like Myers. Then worked in an office at a garage where I met my husband who was a mechanic. Gordon Hibberd, he was a fourth cousin of my adopted family. We married in 1958. I wore a long white dress with a veil and trimmings and had three bridesmaids, two wore apricot long dresses and my Matron of Honour wore peacock blue, there was an argument as the other bridesmaid didn't like the difference. Davina, my best friend was my Matron of Honour and wore glasses. One of the other bridesmaids wanted her to take her glasses off but of course she couldn't see well without them. I said no, she must keep them on.

It was a posh wedding with sixty guests, the reception in a hall near the river. Our honeymoon in London.

We had four children born in England and two more after we moved to Australia. One son has passed away now.

I found all my birth family when I was forty-eight. I have been in contact with them ever since then.

My husband had the most influence on me, he was 11 years older. He enjoyed motor bike riding, but I didn't like it because of the dust. In Australia you just do it on people's properties. He was hopeless at sport, but I liked hockey and swimming. I learnt swimming at school and used to swim in the rivers.

We moved to Australia in 1967. The posters for Australia that we saw at the immigration centre were of bronzed life savers on the sunny beach. Everything looked warm and welcoming. We came to Mudgee, where Gordon had a job at Loneragan's garage through the Trade Commission. Australia had been his first choice whereas I originally thought Canada best.

We came by plane to Sydney, then train to Mudgee. The train was very cold, and it was frosty, we needed foot warmers as it was August. We hadn't thought we'd need coats in Australia. There was a teacher in the carriage who was fascinated by our accents, the children soon lost theirs.

Loneragan's put us up in a hotel until they found us somewhere to rent.

We waited nine years to be naturalised. There was no rush as we could already vote in those days. We knew we would never go back to the UK and like Mudgee the best. Our oldest child was seventeen when we became Australians. We have dual citizenship and have been back to England five times. When we go back dual citizenship is handy to access medical services. We think of ourselves as Aussies.

We lived in Mudgee for twelve years, Gordon built our house. We lived in Emu Plains for twelve years then. When Gordon retired, we bought land at Wollar and lived there for twenty years and now live in Mudgee.

I worked in vineyards and as a nurse's aide in the hospital. Now I enjoy writing and painting and music. I play piano, guitar and the organ. I had lessons for three years but taught myself to play by ear and my teacher didn't like that. I used to go to the Catholic Church when they had Folk Masses. We used to practise in the convent and one day Sister Juliana said, 'Bring your guitar and I will show you a few chords.'

I write by hand, both memories and fiction. I use memories of childhood. I write poetry too and sketch.

Words for my great grandchildren: Have some self-worth and don't put other people down.

My family knows me well. I am an open person.

Chapter 8 – Eileen Rosaleen Csuba

Eileen is a gracious lady, friend to many, and her gift is to spread happiness.

Eileen Csuba

I was born March 1931 at Lidcombe, the eldest of five children. My parents were Clifford Leslie Gersbach and Eileen Cullen (Her name was Sybil May Orford before being adopted.)

My daughter in law took me to the National Library in Canberra and we discovered my grandmother had two illegitimate babies, whom she left when she went to the coast and found their father and had four more children to him.

I have a first memory of my mother sitting in a bedroom laughing at my brother and I who had mumps and fat faces.

I remember when we moved to Ramsgate near the beach. We swam there but had to change into dry clothes quickly so we wouldn't get a cold.

School began at Scarborough Park kindergarten then I went onto St. Pat's at Kogarah. I was addle-brained and was always reading books. There was a cranky old nun, about 70, and then there were lovely nuns, one ran off with one of the Fathers, a big Irishman. I was always in trouble with Mother Superior for forgetting my Child of Mary cape.

I had three sisters and one brother who always tells me he loves me when we hang up the phone, he is now 85.

When he was tiny, we lived near a paddock and he would say to mother, 'Hop over hence into the packet and go to school.'

I had three sisters, but one died at 38 of a cerebral haemorrhage. She was closest to me, the other two were younger and got on well together.

My youngest sister used to say I was her mother.

My first job was as a milliner's apprentice at Kogarah. We used to do renovations on hats. When my boss's husband came back from the war, they opened rooms upstairs and would buy a sample hat and we would copy it. That job lasted 8 years.

I met my husband at the Trocadero, his surname was Czecowsky. We married when I was twenty and my son was born when I was twenty-two, Mark. Then two daughters after that when I was 24, Linda and then 28, Joanne. My husband didn't want children but did love them when they came. I didn't work for seven years then I got a part time job as a salesgirl at Farmers selling upmarket sports clothes. I had several positions selling shoes which I enjoyed.

I divorced after twenty-five years; we were incompatible. He was Czechoslovakian and we had language difficulties and he was a womaniser. I had several attempts at leaving and separation, but I was a Catholic and the priest told me I couldn't leave. A solicitor advised me he could help and get money for me, but I didn't go ahead with him. I was just washing, ironing and looking after the children. I was forty-five.

I met Steve, my second husband at his first wife's second wedding. I had worked with her at Telecom. Her name was Irene but then she changed it to Lyne and is now known as Gypsy. We still keep in touch and rang her the morning of this interview to wish her a happy birthday. I was fifty-one when Steve Csuba and I met, and we were married when I was fifty-two.

Steve and I had Mudgee's Wineglass Bar and Grill for fifteen years and loved it. Steve originally owned it with another person. One memory from then was a toffy nosed woman who was always very nice until she had too much to drink and we'd ask her to leave. I also remember a bikie gang that caused us trouble one day.

By the time I was sixty-three the Health Department were making it very difficult, things like kebabs couldn't be mixed up with one flavour next to another, we had to wear gloves all the time. The business took two years to sell and it broke the marriage of the people who bought it. There were so many excellent places to eat, making it difficult to compete.

When younger I made clothes for myself and my girlfriends. I once made wedding clothes for a bridal party of 8. I could knit but learnt how to do needlework and to crochet at the Mudgee Church Craft Group. I also sang in the View Club Choir.

Steve and I have 8 children between us.

I want my family to know all about me and my life. The birth of my son is a sweet memory, I was in love with him, he is now sixty-six.

For my great great grandchildren, a message. Be kind and love your family and let them know you love them.

Chapter 9 – Kevin James Pye

Kevin is a man of stories and poetry, a sportsman of talent and was a primary school teacher and Principal.

A proud Australian.

Kevin Pye

I was born on 11th August 1943 at Braeholme Private Hospital Mudgee, where Pioneer House is now.

My parents Cecil Pye and Enid Holland, as children lived next door so always knew each other. Enid later became the postmistress at Budgee Budgee.

My great grandfather, John Downing Pye, came to Mudgee in 1868. He built a brick residence at Budgee Budgee in 1884 calling it "Springdale", situated past School Lane on the Cassilis Road. I lived on a mixed farm when young, with a few sheep, cattle, wheat, and orchard—some of the trees still exist and bear fruit, apricots and figs, even after all these years.

My first memory is a photograph of me in the front garden, I remember it being taken by my mother with her Brownie Box camera. I have a lovely curl in my hair. A second early memory is Dad stooking hay and I said to Mum, "I'm going to help Dad stook hay."

I have been married to Narelle for 54 years. I met Narelle when I boarded at her grandmother's place at Croydon Park. Narelle's grandmother was Daisy Cox whose grandfather was John Henry Cox. He jumped ship in Melbourne to go gold prospecting and changed his name to Henry Cox from John Henry Dale

He was friends with Henry Lawson and Henry wrote about him in his books as Harry Dale. Henry's story *The Flour Bin* refers to Cox's farm.

Narelle and I have two children Karen and David. We have five grandchildren and six great grandchildren.

I started school at Mudgee Public School in 1948. A cousin met me at the gate and took me to the Headmistress. I was only in kindergarten for two weeks before I was moved into Year One. I could read. So, I was always the youngest in the class and had to repeat Year Six, as I was only 11 and too young to go the High School. I would have been a farmer, but my Year Six teacher that year was Mr Turner and he inspired me. I had to walk to school along Gladstone Street, which was dirt road in those days. Mudgee now bears no resemblance to what it was when I was a child.

I became Vice Captain of Mudgee High School. I found being in the cadets a most rewarding experience. I was Under Officer during 4th and 5th year at high school. My favourite subjects were the technical ones, but I was good at maths, especially geometry. I wanted to become a manual arts teacher but got a Primary School Scholarship, so became a teacher and loved it. I went to Alexander Mackie College at Paddington and my first appointment was to Mudgee on relief staff in 1963. I lived with Mum and Dad. I travelled as a District Relief Teacher then as a Special Education teacher. Promotion appointments were to Urana Central as Deputy then North Star, Millthorpe, Parkes and Cudgegong Valley all as Principal.

In my first week at Cudgegong Valley School a new kindergarten boy did a 'runner' and was intent on going home. To ensure his safety, the secretary and I followed in my car with him throwing stones back at me. An elderly couple saw the events and called the police thinking they saw something sinister. There were three policemen to learn the truth and enjoy the situation. I wonder what their report said.

I lived for sport, probably one of my downfalls, enjoying tennis, golf, cricket. Other sports I've played are basketball, rifle shooting, athletics and bowls, all of which have trophies on the shelf in my home. I was selected for the Country School Boys coaching class in 1958 at SCG. I played representative cricket wherever I moved once being Vice Captain for Western Districts. I did an Umpires' exam in Parkes in 1988 and was on the Country Representative panel throughout 1990's. I umpired South Africa just before all the strife and could tell the side wasn't getting along.

I umpired West Indies V Australia Country, India, Sri Lanka, Zimbabwe and NZ rep. Teams, Australia V England Women's, NSW V Qld Women's, NSW V Victoria 2nds.

In the NSW Country V Sri Lanka game at Grafton, the Sri Lankan opener, Samaraseka edged a ball onto his thigh pad and it ballooned back towards the bowler who dived forward. My square leg colleague confirmed the catch and I gave him out. The other opener,

Ranatunga, turned to me and said, "You cheat." I asked him to repeat it and he did.

I was pleased a few overs later to adjudge him run out after the bowler deflected a straight drive onto the stumps. I may have even smiled when my finger went up. "Out". Umpire always has his say.

I was appointed State Country Umpires' Advisor, responsible for mentoring and appointing Umpires to representative games. I planned an assessment program involving my observations, captain's reports and self-evaluation to assist the development of top-quality umpires. This involved travel state-wide.

I had success coaching athletics and cricket with the Mudgee Primary Junior girls winning the State Title and Millthorpe girls reaching the final. The Cudgegong Valley boys won the State Cricket Title in 1997. It is marvellous how achievements such as these promote school ethos.

In 2000 I was awarded the Australian Medal for achievements in sport.

I fly the Australian flag outside my home. I am Aussie through and through. I come from convict stock. John Pye was my ancestor, he was transported for stealing malt. I am interested in Australian history and early Australian wares. I have an extensive collection of early Australian glassware and china. Local real estate agents call on me to help with their antique sales. I trade in antiques. I have furniture from my great grandparents that I have tracked down and bought including a beautiful red cedar sideboard made in Australia in 1868.

My third-class teacher, Mr Scott, would sit us on the mat and recite to us. I was fascinated by the rhythm and rhyme. Lawson and Paterson have been a great influence on me also Dud Mills, who presented me with a copy of The Stockwhip and The Spur, with his simple rhymes.

I have written eleven self-published books. E.g. Both Ends Meet in the Middle, Please Read it like I Wrote It, Folklore Matters, Telling Tales, Time is a Traveller (Finalist in Poetry Book of the Year) One for the Road, Lawson Country, Man's Best Friend, All Aboard, Rhythm and Rhyme, The Sepia Soldier.

I have won numerous awards including The Rolf Boldrewood and Queensland Anzac Award. I have won the Tamworth Songwriters Award twice. Jess Holland and Mick Fetch have produced CD's of my lyrics, Mick's "Homecoming" won the Tamworth Songwriters' Encouragement Award.

After retirement in 2000 I grew a flower garden until the drought won the battle with no water in Lawson Creek.

I play bowls now and am the Vice President of the Mudgee Valley Writers.

I work at Mudgee Race Club on a voluntary basis and am timekeeper there. I had a part ownership of a racehorse which did win a race for us. Mudgee Race Club attracts great crowds, bigger than Bathurst or

Orange. I am a Life member of the Mudgee Racing Club, and also life member of Mudgee Cricket Assoc. and Mitchell Zone.

On reflection I think I was meant to be a primary school teacher. I designed the method of integrated programming for the year and was a forerunner of student-centred Learning and Investigation.

I would hope that my great great grandchildren take an interest in their heritage and lead happy and healthy lives.

Chapter 10 – Rachel Adams Knowles

A woman who has the Scottish Fey in her life.

A caring mother who loves all living things.

Rachel Knowles

I was born in Glasgow, Shettleston, Scotland on 1st April 1943. My father, Robert Adams—Adams came from my Dad's side of the family—was also born in Glasgow, as was my mother, Rachel McInnes.

Mum and Dad met at a dance hall; they were both fantastic dancers. They had four children, Catherine, me and John and another wee one, Robert, who died.

We migrated for a better life to Australia in 1951 on the SS Cameronia. I was eight years old. We were sent to the Bonegilla Migrant Hostel at Albury/Wodonga. Dad left for Meadowbank Hostel to look for work. When Mum went into the town to try and find where he was, she broke down crying because the immigration people told her they had never heard of Bobbie Gordon. The Mayor helped her find Dad. It was Christmas time and when we arrived at Meadowbank, we saw big beetles, Christmas beetles, for the first time. We ran around screaming.

I remember the white painted wall and a huge spider on it. Mum hit it many times.

Dad worked in a textile business, *John Vickers*. He used to bring scraps of tartan material home and my table is now covered with a cloth he made from these pieces.

We moved to Dundas and I went to school at Rose Hill primary then high school. We would walk from the

Dundas hostel, over the pipes, to the train station. A farmer on the way would pretend to squeeze milk at us. I didn't like either school.

I realise now that I am dyslexic and wrote backhand and found learning difficult. It held me back and I was very shy. I finished high school and then joined the army when I was seventeen. I wanted to be a driver, but I was only 5'¾" and you had to be 5'1" so I ended up being a cook in the army. In 1964 the Queen and Prince Phillip came to Australia and I was chosen to cook for the Prince. There were three others. I never knew about cheese and thought the cheese in the fridge was off, it had gone green, I threw it out, but the others found it, took it out of the bin and wiped it down. Phillip ate the cheese.

I was in army bases in Mosman, George's Heights, Victoria and Queensland and also in Sydney. When we went on parade there was a little dog who loved me and came on the ground. I was in trouble for that. Someone did a drawing of me and that dog.

I was in the army for six years and was asked four times if I wanted to do courses for promotion, but I thought I wouldn't be good enough and would make a fool of myself. I left with five friends and we travelled Australia in a car together.

As for hobbies, I tried everything. Drawings of family and fairies. Calligraphy, paper art and writing. I've written three songs. Sandy Smith penned the music for

'Mudgee Mudgee', 'Nest in the Hills' and *'The Universal Heartbeat'*.

I joined WIRES and taught others how to rescue and look after animals. I am a snake handler. I rescue and look after sugar gliders and feather tails and bats, I have been vaccinated for the disease they carry. I have a pet roo called Boy.

Leaving WIRES we started a rescue group called the Cudgegong Wildlife Carers (CWC).

I am a medium and in my younger years I was haunted by poltergeists. At Meadowbank Migrants Hostel when I was 9 years old, I saw hundreds of Speed Spiders on my pillow — they were there and in a flash gone.

Then at Dundas Hostel when I was 11 years old to 14 years, I lived with a poltergeist in the room I shared with my little brother John. A hand would come and faces, some gave the feeling of hell and others I felt safe with. Doctors checked me over and word came back to move us out of the room, and it was then used as a mattress storage room.

As a teenager living in Pendle Hill, I woke Mum up telling her Granddad was standing outside under the streetlight looking at us. Mum told me to go to bed I was dreaming — next morning a phone call from Scotland to Mum in Australia saying Granddad had died overnight.

My working life has been varied, nursing homes, crippled children's home in Queensland, and a school for deaf boys.

The man in my life was Bill, he was my boss at a factory called Springs. He looked at me and I looked at him and I said, 'You are my soul mate'. He was 20 years older than me. He told me he was a master locksmith and also a handy man. He was a King Scout and started a group here in Mudgee. We married and have four children, Robert, Timothy, Danny and Travora Kim (a Scottish name) she is called Pebbles. He was a very gentle man and would say to me, 'Rae Rae don't worry. Let it go. I'll wait until you come back, think it over.' He had a sign which said, 'If you can't do it properly don't do it.'

I wasn't a sports person but in the army, I was chosen to swim in an Inter Service Competition. I was a good swimmer, not great though. Someone couldn't take their place in the backstroke. I'd never done it, so they gave me whiskey to make me have a go. I came last.

Over many years we had lots of foster children in our homes. I still have contact with some children via Facebook. They call me Mum. We had rules changed that we saw were wrong in the system. I insisted on being given the history of each child.

Over the years I have completed a Freelance Journalist Course at the Australian College of Journalism. I ran a Youth Centre and volunteered for

Mudgee Vision Impaired. Several other volunteer positions as well.

My whole life is a good memory. No one has the time to think. 'It happened, let it go or you'll never grow.'

I would say to Great Grandchildren 'Take life and run with it but don't punch out other people as you go. Travel along your own road, pick up the memories.'

My farm here at Budgee Budgee is 28 acres and has a dam in the trees that holds eight and a half million gallons. I have rainwater tanks. I don't keep farm animals because I like to see all animals die of old age. I wouldn't sell them.

I would like people to think 'Gee she was a nice person.' And I want to keep writing and illustrating children's books.

Chapter 11 – Annette Frances Fletcher

The village is deep in Annette's soul. Her memories are so vivid today of her family life in Wollar—soon to be lost to coal mining.

Annette Frances Fletcher

I was born in Braeholme Nursing Home Mudgee on 1st October 1945.

My parents:

Leslie Beresford Lang, my father originally from Roma in Queensland then Araluen, Wollar, a 1400 acre farming and grazing property.

Joan Mavis Constable, my mother, came from Merriwa.

I am the eldest of six children.

Good memories are of Christmas at Wollar. Nanna Lang owned the property and her family would all come home, and it was a great time with lots of Christmas gifts and family.

Schooldays began at the Wollar School. There was one teacher, Ron Perry, for forty or fifty children. We walked along the railway siding to get to school and never thought it would be finished. The Sandy Hollow/ Mary Vale Line, it was built during the depression and finished for the mines to take coal to Newcastle.

I then went to Mudgee High School with my two younger sisters. Nanna brought us into Mudgee, and we stayed with an old lady, Mrs. Pedron, in Lovejoy Street, Monday to Friday.

I completed the Intermediate Certificate and then left school and started work where I was able to help out with my family.

On the farm Dad killed our own meat, and we used to milk the cows. We also made our own home-made butter. The Wollar Creek was close to the house to play in, there were large holes, but we weren't allowed to go near them. Leeches were a curse in the creeks. The Fitzpatrick brothers and the Marskell family used to come to visit and play cards, play piano and dance which was just fun. We played 500 and Euchre together too. Mum wasn't a card player but would enjoy sitting by the fire and organising supper with really nice cakes.

We lived without electricity for years. Kerosene lights, an Aladdin lamp for the table at night was wonderfully bright. Bernie Lipka contracted and connected the electricity to Wollar. We had a fuel stove and chip heater and when we were little we used to bath in a big tub by the fire. We all had chores to do. I remember the old black iron to put on the stove to heat, you'd have to rub it clean, then we got Miss Potts irons, with handles. A Silent Knight Kero fridge would be smoking, awful things, useless in summer, frozen solid in winter. We had battery radio.

There was a canvas water bag hanging under the peach tree in the garden for cool water.

Later I worked at the Egg Board in Mudgee, egg grading and office work. The building was opposite the Paragon Hotel.

Then at the Rural Bank but had to resign when I married. Brian Murdoch and I were married in 1967 and we have a son Scott and a daughter Kim.

I was reinstated at the Rural Bank and worked there for eleven years. I was working there when decimal currency came in.

I studied for two years at night at Mudgee TAFE in Short Street, to become a stenographer and I was there when TAFE was flooded. I started work at the Housing Commission in 1978 and finished up there in 2003. Two weeks after I retired, they rang and asked if I would do relief work. I worked at Lithgow and Bathurst three days a week for three and half years. I then worked at reception for Helen Woods. When my brother Beres became sick I decided to retire. I still have many good friends in the Department of Housing. There were many changes especially with computers, fixing problems was difficult.

I married Ron Fletcher in 2003.

Mum and I played A Grade tennis together a lot in Mudgee until I had a water-skiing accident. I played tennis in the Wellington Cup for school sport.

I belong to View Club and also the singing group with Rhonda Brennan. There are twenty-eight in the group. We travel to Gulgong, Dunedoo and Coolah nursing homes and hostels. Sometimes I take residents at Kanandah for a coffee in their new café.

I have been playing the piano since I was six years old by ear. I have played at the Wollar Hall for different functions. I used to play for the CWA in Mudgee. Mum taught her three girls to dance on the back verandah to the Frank Burke White Rose Orchestra as they played on the radio in a half hour program. I love music. When I grew up and moved to Mudgee to work there were beautiful balls, Deb Balls at the Police Boys Club and at Country Comfort as years have gone on. Mum used to dance at the Mechanics Institute hall, and she played the mouth organ right up to her death.

My mum and I were very close, she was not quite 18 when I was born. She never left town. We sang and danced together. We had our last dance three weeks before she died. We were at the Soldiers Club and she asked for *The Tennessee Waltz* to be played and we danced together. She died in April 2011 at 84. Dad has been gone for twenty-three years.

The village of Wollar was first declared on 20th March 1885. William Lawson came through in 1822 and first mentioned the Goulburn River. The Kamilaroi people were the original inhabitants.

Mum's parents are buried in the Wollar cemetery and Dad's are buried in the Mudgee Cemetery. I call out to the village to check the old house out from time to time; it is still there but been purchased by the mines.

Originally the property was sold to Security Estates and subdivided into 25-acre blocks. There are still two churches, St. Luke's Anglican and St. Lawrence's, Catholic. They are no longer used. There is a small cemetery behind the Anglican Church that closed in 1950's, the General Cemetery is past the school. There used to be a general store, bakery, post office, police station, tennis courts, cricket club and a school. The police station closed in 1966 and the post office in 1978. They also had picnic races which were held at Wandoona—owned by the Singles. There are memories of the green bin of dry ice to keep the ice cream cold at the picnics.

When the Wollar Post Office closed we then got a mail service from Ulan. Les Griffiths was the mailman, he brought mail, bread and whatever else was needed (including Dad's alcohol). The road to Mudgee was all gravel until tar arrived in 1997. My sister got car sick every trip to Mudgee.

There is a funny memory, funny now, of riding our uncle's fixed wheel bike home from school one day after collecting high top loaves of bread. We were coming downhill towards the ramp, carrying two loaves of bread. I was sitting on the seat, Cheryl was on the bars and Jenny was peddling. We hit the side of the ramp, fell off, bodies and mail and bread went everywhere. We were knocked about and got into trouble when we got home. Definitely no sympathy.

I would like my family to know their history and to stay connected. It is a shame today that families move away and lose touch. And for my great great grandchildren to have love and respect for one another and to have a nice healthy and happy life like I have had.

Chapter 12 – Maureen Fae Scifleet

A life wish to be a nurse. Never anything else. Collecting dolls, a hobby that began as a child. "Collecting is the most important part of being a collector."

Fae Scifleet

I was born in Newcastle on 20th July 1932. My parents both came from there. Dad worked in a factory and my mother didn't go out to work. She and her mother and sister were seamstresses. I am the middle child of three girls.

School was at a private school at Cooranbong, Newcastle. I did a tertiary education course in Science to help with my nursing training.

My first memory is when I was about eighteen months old and we moved into a new house. I distinctly remember leaving one house and then going through a gate to the new one.

When the last of my children started school, I did my General Nursing and then I went to the Mater, Crows Nest, in 1971 for 12 months to do Midwifery, then to Petersham in 1980 to do Tresillian, child and family health. I also worked at the Royal Hospital for Women in Paddington.

I was Nursing Unit Manager in the Maternity Section of Mudgee District Hospital. It was very busy with sixteen beds. When I left the hospital in 1990, I did ten years at the Baby Health Centre Clinic, which was situated where the Information Centre is now. I did clinics in Ulan, Bylong, Wollar, Hargraves and Lue, once or twice a month and weekly in Gulgong. Home visits sometimes in outlying areas. There were no mobile phones and when I had to go to night calls, I would take my husband with me in case I needed a car mechanic.

I would give injections, advice on seat belts, watch the babies' development and all things to do with a young baby. There were records to keep and a lot of writing. Then they brought in computers and it was necessary to put in all kinds of stats. I was nursing from when you had to wash everything by hand. There was a wash basin in every room. When disposables were brought in everything changed.

In the new hospital system, there is a problem in that the mothers are anxious to go home with the new baby but there is often no-one to check things like breasts and nipples, blood loss and baby. No one checks for three days until the District Midwife comes.

University training in comparison to training in hospitals—there are things for both ways. When a girl left school at sixteen or seventeen, she went straight to hospital to start nursing. She would see everything; emergencies and the treatment would be explained to the junior nurse so next time she would know what to get and how to treat. Now a group of girls and their leader come from Uni and talk while teaching should be done. When working in a hospital you see things and learn how to handle things and what people say to other people, when you come from Uni and only work two or three weeks a year in a hospital you do not have these skills and have no idea how to talk to someone who is distressed etc. Modern technology is the way of nursing these days.

My husband, William Jeffrey Scifleet, and I met at The Sanitarium Hospital where he was a masseur. He was from Mudgee and we came here in 1952 and had all our six sons here, including two sets of twins. I was young and fit and a good organiser. Now I don't have any family in Mudgee. They are scattered all over the place, my nearest son is three hours away. I have nine grandchildren and seven great grandchildren.

When I was young, I played basketball and was a good runner. When I lived in Newcastle one of the teachers from school was an instructress in Folk Dancing. I enjoyed that and went to the Gym. We often dressed up and had concerts where we dressed up in fancy costumes made of coloured crepe paper, with rows of petals and decorated hats. My mother was good at making things like that, it kept us busy.

My boys played football but were more interested in motor bikes when they were young.

I love reading and doll collecting has been important part of my life. It's the collecting not the collection — the chase is the exciting part. I used to go to markets when away at nursing seminars and seek out dolls. People who knew I collected would ring me and tell me where there was a doll for sale. I like rag dolls, and it took me a long time to find dolls that I liked as a child. When I was a little girl, I would see photos of American dolls like Shirley Temple. I have Australian ones that I treasure, they are more valuable than the American ones. I dress the dolls myself, knit their cloths and my sister did crochet, and tatting and smocking some of the clothes.

I joined and ran the Armchair Travel Course at U3A. It was run from the old TAFE building in Short Street then moved to Adams Street Hall. I would make afternoon tea to be enjoyed by all, the men like the sweet cakes. I did the Current Affairs Course as well. I used to like cooking but now my hands have seized up and I can't do it. I am enrolled in the Current Affairs and Eastern History courses this year with U3A. I have travelled to Norfolk Island and Tasmania and most states of Australia but, as my husband didn't like to travel, I didn't go overseas.

I was Commandant in the Voluntary Aide Detachment in Mudgee which was associated with the Red Cross and popular in the 1960's. We had a group of about thirty girls who did First Aide, home nursing and worked at the hospital helping with patients, all on a voluntary basis. We would march in uniform on Anzac Day and the records are now all kept at the museum. The organization was begun during the First World War as the Voluntary Aide Detachment. Mrs. Persia Portia was the Grand Lady in Sydney and she came up and we staged mock accidents in the park. We would make up the participants, Dr Barr would be there as he was doctor for the department, and we would transport patients to the hospital, rooms would have been vacated, the Matron and nurses would be in attendance and people would pretend to be hysterical looking for lost relatives. This group lasted about ten years and then I went back to nursing until I retired in 1999 when my husband became ill. I am now a Curator of the Colonial Inn Museum. I decided to work in a field totally different to nursing.

My cat, Wow, came here to me starving and I fed her for about six months, now she is here to stay. She is a Rag Doll cat and is good company.

One memory that I hold close is when I gave a party for my older sister when she turned eighty and my younger sister seventy, here in my home. My eldest son was here too and it was a really enjoyable day.

A message of wisdom from a baby health nurse, I learnt a lot about young people having babies and found it so much better for young mothers to enjoy their babies before they go to preschool and school.

"Enjoy your baby while you have them and you are their centre person."

Chapter 13 – Ross Leslie Kurtz

A music man, artist, collector, farmer and to top it all off, a pushbike rider extraordinaire.

Ross Kurtz

I was born in the Mudgee Hospital on 24th April 1950, Anzac Day. Doctor Carter missed the service for the first time because of me.

My father Reginald Roland Kurtz was born at Braeholme Private Hospital Mudgee. He was a farmer and apiarist. My mother, Rita June Holland, was born in Honeysuckle near Weetaliba, and worked before her marriage at the Jeldi factory in Mudgee where the PCYC is now.

I am the eldest of their two sons, my brother Bruce is 16 months younger.

Living in the little house at the top end of the Avondale property is my first memory. Cold in winter with the wind whistling through the weatherboards and boiling hot in summer. There were few trees around the cottage, one apricot tree that is still there beside the house.

I went to Mudgee Public School on the Ulan bus driven then by Wally Trantor. I didn't like school. When I was about ten years old, I attended the Cooyal School for a short time as the teacher was boarding with our family. Then back to Mudgee School. I obtained the Intermediate Certificate at the High School.

Dad bought *Glenroy*, which had been owned by my grandfather, Alf Kurtz, and my uncle. My grandmother on my father's side was a Roth. I planted grapes in 1969.

I was a jack-of-all-trades and overseered the vineyard and workers on Gil Walchrist's Botobolar Vineyard for a time, he was editor of the Mudgee Guardian then.

Music came into my life early. I remember going to sleep to songs written and sung by my dad, and when we were adults, I would go to sleep with Dad playing the fiddle. I realize now they were lullabies. Those thoughts bring me great pleasure today. If Dad was here today and playing, I could still nod off. Dad taught me to play the tin whistle, Fred Holland, my maternal grandfather played music with my uncles. I am sensitive to the importance of the folk music of this area. Folk music has been handed down from generation to generation and played by people sitting around enjoying music and the company. I like the words "Folk Gathering" used by Goulburn folk groups, it sounds the more laid-back style.

Dad, Bruce and I were asked to join a group of Gulgong musicians, The Gold Diggers, to raise money to rebuild the Gulgong Opera House. Frank Halloran was the instigator, a journalist with the Mudgee Guardian, he was killed before his time. Then we decided to form the family Stringy Bark Band in about 1969, named after the poem by Henry Lawson, "The Stringy Bark Tree." We played at the Cooyal Hall, and in Mudgee, Dubbo, Orange, Bathurst and Walgett, for birthday parties and weddings. One memorable venue was the Beecroft Community Centre where 200 people gathered and danced with enthusiasm. Another time we played in front of Government House in Sydney. Often we played with the Home Rule Bush Band.

John Meredith collected folk music from around Australia, Irish, British and German songs, mining and wool industry tunes, he took them back to Sydney where folk music had a renaissance. Roving people like my grandfather had concertinas because they were easy to carry around. I play a 12-string guitar, tin whistle and lagerphone—made from bottle tops from lager bottles. My roots are in bush music. I do love classical music and had four years classical voice training which helps me to sing, it gives me the tools. I write songs and poems now.

As a hobby I collect tractors, all sorts and sizes. Massey Ferguson 35 I think is the best of them.

I built a shed for us to live in while I built the house. My house I built from timber from friends' properties. I cut the timber, barked the logs and brought the large round timber home. The mud bricks were made here from clay just down the paddock. I made a crane to lift the large logs. It took me 11 years to build our home and studio.

I have been painting for forty years and I teach art. Plein air is the way I enjoy painting most. I like to capture the light starting to move towards reaching inside the landscape, colours, monitoring the essence of the light. A little bit abstract, strong colours characterize and emphasize colour. Landforms are very feminine around here. I spent some years painting in oils but work in acrylics and watercolours now, combining watercolour and oil in acrylics. I used to copy Jolliffe to learn to draw trees. I like pen drawing. Salt Bush Bill a favourite.

Tennis has been my sport. I played around the area, Cooyal, Ulan, Moolarben and Mudgee. My parents played on those courts, we kids roamed the bushlands surrounding the courts. Cec Garling's courts were a favourite.

I ride a pushbike. One winter recently I rode 2,000 kms from Darwin to Broome in temperatures of 35 degrees. It was to raise money for the Royal Flying Doctor Service, eight of us rode, Mudgee folk and friends from Lightning Ridge. Judy, my wife, drove the backup vehicle.

I married Judy in 1991, having met her at the Mitchell College art tutorials. I have three children from my first marriage to Ruth, two girls and a son. Now I have nine grandchildren and two great grandchildren.

One of the most important people in my life is Gil Walchrist, a journalist, he was good with words. I used to hang on his every word, I was a simple country kid whom he employed on his vineyard. My dad loved a sense of the ridiculousness in words. When young he told me they had a church service at Botobolar, in the house of two spinster sisters. They always cooked a pudding for supper after the service and once when they weren't expecting the service to be at their house they told everyone—"No pudding Sonny, we's weren't repaired." The way people spoke—not educated, not hearing the words properly.

I am a Henry Lawson tragic; he often wrote in the style of the way people spoke. 'Howsomenever' my uncle would say, it means 'well, anyway.' I am in fear of a lot of our language being lost with all the texting. A play on words and sense of ridiculous, you can't capture it. There is no-one to have rapport with, it is lonely, with a phone the whole of life. I am thinking of writing a song about a lonely girl with a hand on her phone, but lonely. A sad song. It isn't a valid form of communication; it came too quick. It scares people, they are frightened. I remember horses on the property and now—I think we were the luckiest generation. I missed the Vietnam ballot. I wouldn't have gone anyway; it wasn't our war.

I have 'trod the boards' at the Town Hall Theatre with Mudgee Performing Arts Society and Gulgong MADS. I played Billy Brigalow in a musical *Fiddler on the Roof* with Ken Charter who was so supportive of me, the new kid on the block. I went on to star in Gilbert and Sullivan's *Ruddigore*, also *Circus Anyone?* and *Joe Wilson's Courtship*. I find acting nerve wracking, remembering the lines! I was on the Cudgegong Southbank Committee and had a plan of having a stage built over the river. The Town Hall Theatre isn't made for good audience viewing. We do have a sports centric council unfortunately.

The dearest memory I have is of our first house, not very comfortable, but we could experience the four seasons, cold winters, hot summers and only 2000 gallons of rainwater. Baths in an inch of water. You felt nature. Now people are so far out of touch with nature. I love studying birds and being out there in touch with Mother Nature. People now find the use of animals abhorrent, but it is the way of nature. With the increased global warming and population, we need to find other ways to produce food. The grazing of animals may not be sustainable in the future, areas of the ground are becoming bare, areas I have never seen before, bare. Insects can be processed into flour. My niece's husband exports food into Asia. So, we think we can find a market there for insects.

I have a good handle on family history and the older I get I understand the pain indigenous people had. They were part of Mother Nature, their pain must have been horrendous, to be ripped from their land.

Wise words for my great great grandchildren would be to respect your heritage, from that can come all wisdom.

Chapter 14 – Heather Valma Rushton

A world traveller, adventurer, a teller of tales in words and photography.

Heather Rushton

I was born at the King George Hospital in Camperdown on 27th October 1956, the eldest of the three children of William Owen Rushton and Valma Doris Keep who had known each other since early childhood.

They were children of the Great Depression and lived on a settlement block at Hammondville outside Liverpool, Sydney. It was built under the auspices of Cannon Hammond (St Barnabas, Broadway) to accommodate poor families with three or more children. Each family was given a one-acre block on which to build a house and produce food. The men were expected to build the houses as employment. There was a kitchen and two bedrooms, a combustion stove and a tap out the back in the lean-to bathroom/laundry. As my Aunt put it, "as children we didn't know what we were missing because no one had anything".

When my parents married, they built a house at Macquarie Fields, long before it became a Housing Commission suburb. Dad's workplace had to provide the home loan as the bank considered Macquarie Fields was too far out of Sydney. Dad was a window dresser and ticket writer for W.H. Soul Pattinson's chemist. He became friends with young apprentice pharmacists and continued that friendship when they set up agencies around the city. One of those men eventually moved to Coonabarabran, so once a year Dad would fly up to

Coonabarabran, usually at the time of the Coona Cup, towards Christmas to decorate his friend's shop.

Mum's work had been in the clerical field, but she became a stay at home mum and after my brother was born, she learnt cake decorating at Tech and continues to produce cakes to this day.

When I was fifteen, Dad decided to move us to Coonabarabran. I didn't want to go, but within twelve months I had become a country girl and still am.

My first memory was when we were visiting friends who lived on the harbour. They had a two-storey house and I remember dragging their toys down the stairs (and getting into trouble for doing that).

I began school at Macquarie Fields Public School, then attended the High School at Ingleburn till third form, completing my secondary education at Coonabarabran High. After that I won a Teacher's Scholarship and went to Armidale University where I lived in the Mary White College which I loved.

My first posting as a teacher was to Dunedoo Central School as a Supernumerary which meant that I could be moved to wherever there was a vacancy. After six months I was moved back to Coonabarabran and had my little brother in my class. After returning to Dunedoo for two years I took 12 months leave and headed overseas. Before departing I had filed my preference for a posting with the Department of Education, nominating anywhere in the Western or North Western school districts, but had stipulated

"NOT Moree." On my return to Australia my brother-in-law rang and asked if I liked my new posting (which I had not seen at that point). He said, "It starts with an M and ends with two EE's". Fortunately for me it was Mudgee.

I taught English and History at Mudgee High for eight years and then became Head Teacher English at Kandos High School for twelve years before returning to MHS as Head Teacher Administration. During that time, I also acquired a Masters of Education in Creative Arts.

My theatre career began with a non-speaking role in first class, playing the duck in Peter and the Wolf where I was ignominiously eaten by the wolf. In second class I was a bird in a play and still remember my line, "Twitter twitter, it makes me want to sing."

At Macquarie Fields I joined the Girls Brigade at the Baptist Church and learnt, among many other skills, to recite poetry and perform. I played a salty sea captain in the school musical in sixth class and at Ingleburn High took part in Gilbert and Sullivan productions. This trend continued at Coonabarabran High where I was in The Mikado. Although I have belonged to numerous choirs and singing groups, I have never had any formal singing training.

I was also a member of the Coonabarabran Dramatic Society. Probably my most memorable role was in Neil Simon's Plaza Suite, where I played a bride who had locked herself in the bathroom and refused to come out for her wedding. This production was taken out to the Warrumbungle National Park where, at that time, there was a prison farm. You have no idea the number of proposals I received from inmates on that day.

One of the first things I did when I arrived in Mudgee was to join the Mudgee Dramatic Society. My first role was in a play called Love Rides the Rails, staged in the Civic Theatre. It was a melodrama and as the heroine I had to remove my bright red skirt (shock, horror) to flag down the approaching train. It was the first of many roles in productions over the years, the most challenging being Lady Windermere in Lady Windermere's Fan.

In 1985 the Dramatic Society merged with the Musical Society and the Opera Trust to form Mudgee Performing Arts Society with Ken Charter as President. After 10 years he stepped aside, and I took up the reigns almost continuously for the next 20 years.

I love the magic of theatre. I enjoy directing and occasionally writing a short play. Putting on a play is a team effort, so you will find me doing all sorts of jobs like operating front of house, running the canteen, managing backstage, anything with Mudgee Performing Arts Society.

My hobbies are more obsessions, travel and photography. My first overseas trip was to New Zealand for a Jamboree with the Girls Brigade. Next it was to London where, at Heathrow, I met a teacher from Melbourne. We travelled around England visiting her relatives and are still friends. Together we travelled through Europe on a Contiki Tour for nine weeks. It was before the European Union, so I got a taste of each city, borders with passports and changing currencies. It was a good way to travel with young people.

The most important person in my life has been Sandy Smith who I met in the principal's office (Kevin Hefferen) on my first day in Mudgee High School. We were among the seven new teachers appointed to MHS in 1983. Sandy had been at Parkes High School and was returning to the classroom after three years as the Arts Consultant for the Western District. I soon realized this was a person who shared interests similar to me; theatre, music, travel, photography and words. Sandy was an extremely intelligent and capable woman. She built up the band and music at the High School and together we directed three musicals for MHS and three musicals for MPAS along with numerous theatre restaurants and other productions.

Our first trip together was to Western Australia, crossing the Nullarbor in Sandy's Corolla Station wagon, camping and staying with friends and relatives along the way. Sandy said, "If you can travel with someone you can almost live with them." But it took another five years and many more travel adventures before I was invited to move in.

Our first overseas trip in 1986/7 was a five-week journey from Hong Kong to London by train, passing through China, Mongolia, Siberia, Russia and the

Eastern European counties. It was an Intrepid Tour from which everyone else had pulled out because of the disaster at Chernobyl so there was no guide, just the two of us being met at each location by government tourist agents. This led to an amazing experience.

My play tells it all:

Do You Speak Englis?

A sleeper carriage of a train. Two women sitting upright, opposite each other on the lower bench seats. Both are looking at the door of the carriage. At the sound of the door slamming shut, they both slump back on the seats.

S: (*relieved*) We've done it. We've got away with it.

H: Dunno. That last guy wasn't happy. Maybe they've gone to get a woman to do a **thorough** search…

S: (*standing shaking the front of her top*) I'm sweating in places I've never sweated before.

H: Open the window—that'll soon cool you down.

(*S moves to down stage left, H to down stage right. They take turns to address the audience*)

S: Cool, that's an understatement—it was minus 10 degrees outside.

H: It was 1987, very much in the Soviet era, and we were nearing the end of a great adventure, Hong Kong to London by train.

S: The tour group we were meant to be with had dwindled to just us, (beat) Chernobyl blowing up a few months before may have had something to do with that—

H: And it was the middle of Winter—

S: (*Turning to H*) Well, who wants to see Siberia in Summer?

H: up till then, the coldest Winter they'd had since WWII. There was so much snow that the railway line was being cleared with dynamite-

S: Which is why the train was delayed crossing into Mongolia and we arrived at Ulan Bator having already lost a day.

H: We were met and taken to a dark, echoing Russian built hotel. The next morning…

(S and H move centre stage and a Mongolian woman in a suit enters to join them)

Guide: You liked the soup last night? It had lots of goose fat. Goose fat keep you warm, and good for your skin (*patting her cheeks*). Your accommodation, it is not paid for. You pay?

S: No worries. Our Travel Agent has given us a bank cheque (*produces it from her bag*).

Guide: (*looking horrified*) No. No good. We do not take cheques.

S: But it's a bank cheque, not a personal one.

Guide: (*firmly*) We do not take cheques. You pay now?

(S & H return to the front of the stage)

H: Pay now? Great idea, but our money was in traveller's cheques and (*mimicking the guide*) they did not take cheques.

S: What to do? We didn't fancy spending the rest of our lives in a Mongolian gaol so we did what any antipodean would do when in strife—we called on the British.

(British Consul enters the middle area. S & H join him)

Consul: Nice day for a walk out there?

H: We could do with some ice spikes to deal with those frozen paths.

Consul: I'll do what I can but that's not much. You will have to pay the bill with what money you have and I'll contact the Australian Embassy in Moscow to let them know you're on the way. By the way, you wouldn't happen to know the latest cricket score would you?

(S & H address the audience again)

S: Poor bloke. He didn't get much news out there.

H: He gave us his interpreter, the use of the ambassadorial Land Rover and we headed to the bank with our mixed currency traveller's cheques, but

S&H: They 'do not take cheques'

(Female bank employee enters the central area)

Bank employee: *(reading the traveller's cheques)* This says 'Commonwealth Bank of Australia', and British pounds. *(looking at S & H)* But Australia has dollars. *(triumphantly)* This is not right.

(S & H address the audience)

H: Eventually they accepted them, leaving us with one American Express cheque for $20 (which we couldn't cash) to get us to Moscow, two weeks away.

S: The next morning we were back on the train having seen nothing more of Ulan Bator than the hotel and bank.

H: When we crossed into the Soviet Union we thought we'd be able to cash that remaining cheque

S: But nyet! In the one sled town where we tried, our cheque did not match the no doubt outdated picture of a traveller's cheque they had pinned to the wall of the office.

H: The train continued across the frozen expanses of Siberia. Irkurtzk and Novisibirsk, were wonderful and, fortunately, the accommodation and breakfasts were paid for in advance. It's amazing how much food one can stuff into the pockets of a large coat.

S: Our cabin attendant was a charming elderly man who took pity on us when he realized we had no money for the dining car meals, and so brought us 'waffly' biscuits with our glasses of tea.

H: We finally reached Moscow and the Australian embassy.

Ambassador enters to central space S& H join him.

A: The agency has sent through the money you've been waiting for.

S: Yipee! Now we can eat!

A: You realise that you're going to have to hide this money because you didn't declare it when you arrived in Russia.

(S+H address the audience)

H: The only way to raise that sort of money in Russia at that time was to have been operating on the black market or standing on street corners.

S&H: (*Turn and look each other up and down*) I don't think so.

S: So between Moscow and the Polish border many hundreds of dollars disappeared into our underwear and our entry papers were 'adjusted'.

The guard enters

J: You have papers?

He looks suspiciously at them, then at us, then leaves in silence.

S: (*relieved*) We've done it. We've got away with it.

H: Dunno. That last guy wasn't happy. Maybe they've gone to get a woman to do a **thorough** search…

S: (*standing shaking the front of her top*) I'm sweating in places I've never sweated before.

H: Open the window—that'll soon cool you down.

(Sharp rapping on the door and it opens to reveal a large, uniformed Russian woman. S&H look at her and gulp)

H: (*to audience*) She was enormous. Resistance was futile. It would be a full body search, for sure.

W: You speak Englis?

S+H: (*S& H look at each other in horror*) Yes…

W: You will help me with my Englis homework?

Blackout

Over the next 27 years, Sandy and I travelled extensively, visiting all seven continents and over 100 countries. Much of that travel was with Colin Sale who led tours for the Geographical Society of NSW. Being 'veterans' of his tours, when Colin retired, he handed the mantle of tour manager to Sandy and me. Sadly, Sandy passed away in early 2014 before the first tour happened, but I have had the privilege of leading eight tours for the Society.

Memories to hold forever are the places I experienced with Sandy, especially Antarctica in 2010. I love Antarctica.

The special wisdom I'd like to pass on is:

"Life is short. Get out and do things."

Chapter 15 – Joyce Mildred Purtle

A much talented Joyce Purtle, her story is filled with her many activities.

A woman of action.

Joyce Purtle

I was born in Mudgee at Broughton Private Hospital in Short Street on 27th July 1945 after my father had gone around the rabbit traps and made the slow journey into town.

My parents were Cyril Ernest Baker, who was also born at the same hospital in Short Street and Gwendolyn Florence Edith Patch who came from Eulo, where her parents owned the Hotel. They met while Dad was shearing there, and they were married in Dubbo. I am the eldest child and have twin sisters and a brother.

My father began as a shearer and over his lifetime managed to accumulate over 4,000 acres of land. He was on Cudgegong Shire Council for twenty-five years and became Shire President and held many other offices. Baker's Lane and the bridge over Linburn Creek are named after him.

I have an early memory of our house—my grandfather built it at Linburn, and it is still very functional, admittedly with additions 113 years later. There were my parents, Dad's father, Mother's parents and we four children all living in a one-bedroom house. Everyone slept in sleep-outs and verandahs. We had a very happy childhood. I remember going up the paddock in a wagonette with my grandfather cutting down trees to make yards and catching rabbits. He was our much-loved baby-sitter. We never had much money, but we had the best life.

I went to school on Wally Tranter's Ulan bus to Mudgee—it cost five shillings a week. My best friends on the bus were Naomi Leven, Jeanette Cross, Neva Webb and Elsie Bowles. In Infants I was taught by Miss Kellett—her father planted the Kurrajong trees out to the cemetery. In 5th class Mrs Edna Wells proved an excellent teacher. In 6th class I went to St Gabriel's School in Waverley, Sydney which was conducted by Anglican Sisters. I completed the Leaving Certificate in 1962. I wanted to be a teacher but didn't get a scholarship. In those days you had to gain one to go on to Teacher's College. I then spent a year at home, it was the best year of my life being involved with all farm activities and renovating the family home. Mrs Hulme taught me shorthand and typing at Mudgee TAFE. I went on to teach typing at Mudgee TAFE and later Typing and English at Collarenebri Central School even though I wasn't qualified to do so until years later.

My first job was at the Housing Commission when Eric Reddington was in charge. The office was where Outside the Square Coffee Shop is now. Personal problems necessitated a move to Head Office in Sydney where I worked as a secretary to a Parliamentary Liaison Officer. That was boring, so I went on to work at the Readers Digest and Sydney University. I decided nursing was for me. I was enrolled at RPA but thought I was too old at nineteen. I was nervous living in Sydney and decided to apply for a governess's job. I answered four positions advertised in "The Land" and the "Country Life" and the Cutler family, living thirty miles out of Collarenebri accepted me—they had two children. No one met me at Pokataroo, so I went with the mailman in a beaten-up old truck. The Cutler family had a flat tyre and were late. I had to open fifteen gates in my stockings and high heels, and it was so hot in late January. I stayed at Blantyre for one year and met my husband, Michael, on the first day. He was working on the family property next door and came to check me out. He had six other girlfriends at that time, so it was interesting until he decided which one he liked best. His mother, who he was very close to said, 'I don't know my young shaver, but she is far too good for you.' That decided him! She had also gone to St Gabriel's. Her mother didn't attend her wedding, as she didn't approve of her daughter's husband being a boundary rider. I had the best of times as a governess and going to Balls and tennis parties around the area. I did sewing and knitting for myself and my friends. I came home for Christmas after leaving Collarenebri. Michael's brother offered me a job in his Stock and Station office and my father asked why I would want to go back there. Michael had asked me to marry him.

I married Michael Jackson Purtle in 1968 at St John's Church of England in Mudgee and had the reception at the CWA rooms. The photographer got bogged on the way from Collarenebri so we had no photos. A local photographer did take some studio photos, but he absconded and some three years later police found him, and we were able to obtain a few wedding photos.

We lived with Michael's parents for three years. Michael and I bought the school bus and I drove it thirty miles twice a day from the "Eight Mile" where we lived to the Queensland border along the Mungindi road and back into Collarenebri. When it rained only ten points on that dirt road the bus couldn't go anywhere. I remember getting bogged and having to walk five miles to the nearest house for help.

Another day I LOST the motor—it just fell out. Another time the wheel came off on that rough gravel road. I had to dodge kangaroos and emus. The children were generally well behaved and practised their spelling and tables.

Then we bought the old family home, which had been bought by the CWA as a home for mothers awaiting the birth of babies. School teachers also boarded there. Michael bought Cloey's garage workshop and sold and repaired cars. Our children were born after we moved to town—Patrick, Matthew and Jessica. There was everything for them in Collarenebri: swimming club, cubs, scouts, music and ballet lessons and the best school.

We moved to Mudgee in 1987 after my dad died. We came home to manage the property at Linburn. We had a few cattle, but mainly merino sheep and first cross lambs.

My husband Michael became the most important person in my life.

The children worshipped him. He could make friends with anyone. He had a brilliant mind. He was very involved with the Masonic Lodge, as were his father and brother and the running of Collarenebri Rodeo, Race Club and War Memorial Club. Michael loved parties and going to the races in Sydney and to Bourke and beyond. We had shared a racehorse, The Scotsman, a beautiful black horse who won the Opal Bracelet for us in Lightning Ridge. Michael was a bookmaker and I enjoyed the races too. A friend, Ernie Smith, did the bag at the races. He came to visit us for a weekend and stayed four years. All our family and friends were devastated when Michael succumbed to a brain tumour in October 2003. A wonderful life cut short.

A memory I hold dear is when I organised my daughter Jessica's wedding. There were 300 guests at St John's and a reception at the Police Boys Club. It was a huge undertaking making the bridal party dresses, the cake, and supervising all the catering and decorating. Ironing the damask tablecloths was a mammoth task. I did hire four ladies to serve and wash up.

I have compiled a book of my mother's poetry, written a book on Cooyal, and The Baker Family, also books on Gold Mining at Linburn and another on William Oxley, an ancestor. I am currently writing my life story and compiling a history of the Purtle Family in Collarenebri.

Both in Collarenebri and in Mudgee I have always been known for my catering and involvement in many organizations. At Collarenebri: Central School P. & C., Red Cross, C.W.A., Rodeo, Swimming Club, Scouts, Brownies, Anglican Women's Guild. Over the past 30 years I have been an office bearer in the Cooyal Hall Association, Cooyal Park Trust, Mudgee N.S.W. Farmers' Association and St. Gabriel's Old Girls Union. I have also had long involvement with other associations such as the St. Andrew's Anglican Church at Cooyal, the Cooyal Bush Fire Brigade and the Mudgee U3A. Community is so important.

My auntie was a Catholic nun in Brisbane and sent me a holy card when I was about twelve it said:

"God's Minute"

I have only just one minute

Only sixty seconds in it,

Forced upon me can't refuse;

Didn't seek it, didn't choose it;

I must suffer if I lose it,

Give account if I abuse it,

Just a tiny little minute —

But Eternity is in it."

She said learn this and you won't waste a minute.

Running our farm, involvement with my children's families and voluntary work leaves little time for a wasted minute. This is something that I would like to pass onto my eight grandchildren.

Chapter 16 – Malcolm William Roth

Mudgee wine runs in Malcolm's veins. A talented farmer with many interests.

Malcolm Roth

I was born in the old Mudgee Hospital 26th August 1938.

My father, William Clive Roth, was a Mudgee man and mother, Zillah Maude Williams, came from Home Rule, located just north of Mudgee. My mother was a wonderful woman. I had an older brother, Don and a younger sister Elaine. I am fourth generation of wine makers, the first being Adam Roth, then William, my father William and now me.

Dad bought Westcourt in 1927 and when he died, he left it to his elder grandson, I bought it back in 1994. In 1908 Westcourt became a racing stud. In 1915 the horse Westcourt ran in the Melbourne Cup where it came second and broke down but recovered and ran in The Cup again in 1917 in which it won. The second horse from the stud, Eastcourt, came in 7th in the race. Bucholtz and Frederickbergs owned Westcourt prior to Danny Seaton who set up the racing stud. Then the Roth family bought it in 1927. There are records in the Mudgee Museum about these people and the size of the vineyards, at one stage the biggest in the southern hemisphere (260 acres). The grape industry commenced just before the turn of the century when gold mining disappeared. There were 30,000 people here in the Gold Rush Days. The district diversified into wool, cereal grains, lucerne and prospered.

Our grapes grown here on my property are processed locally. Our Cellar Door building is just finished, and we are in the process of fitting it out ready for an opening. It is 87 Westcourt Lane, Eurunderee. We have designed distinctive labels for our wines.

I was six when I started school at the Eurunderee School. I attended for six years without missing one day. I loved school. When I started there fourteen or fifteen children attended. I rode my pushbike to High School in Mudgee, but Dad would pick me up if it was raining. The frosts were so heavy in winter the lapels on my coat would be white with frost. The Farm Mechanics and the Agricultural Block were my favourites at High School.

I raised pigs at one stage and used to milk cows and separate the milk for them. I milked the cows wherever they stood, didn't use a bail, would give them a handful of hay. They came when I called them from grazing along the creek. One day I heard a noise in the gravel of the creek, it was a huge King Brown snake. I killed it with a stick and hung it on the fence. I told Dad about the snake and when he went to get the Mudgee Newspaper there was a photo of my snake on the front page hanging over onto the ground from both sides of the fence. 8 foot 6 inches long. Some folk had been sampling wine at Craigmoor and seeing the snake, took the photo. Since that time, I have changed my thinking about snakes. I don't worry about the black ones, but I do about the browns, with children around the house.

There are people now who come and catch them and move them on.

For 71 years I have been involved in the wine industry beginning work when I was 10 at Eurunderee. I helped at Craigmoor Wines with pruning and with the cherry trees. In my younger years besides working with wines I went shearing and I share farmed wheat all over the district. I went to shearing school at Armatree— Hamilton Park, owned by the Cox's and did 100 sheep a day by the end of my first week. Most sheds I contracted on my own but did do some work with shearing contractors Sid Williams and Joe Considine. When hail destroyed wheat crops, I could always earn a living shearing.

Margaret Ellen Walsh and I married in 1961 and we have three children and now 5 grandchildren. I hope the grandchildren will follow the family in the wine industry.

I have always had time for sport. Especially tennis and cricket, and I was good at hockey. Bowls has been my sport in my latter years. Being the former President of the Bowling Club I am sad they have pulled down the old club in Burrundulla Avenue.

I have had many hobbies in my life, wine making being just one. I was a member of the Junior Farmers that later became Rural Youth. The Junior Farmers was a good foundation for the future of being a successful farmer. Bee keeping one of the activities then, I no longer have hives, as the American Brood Disease drove me from that interest. I have been Vice President of Mudgee Show Society in the 70's. Gough Whitlam visited the show when I was Chief Steward, and I had the privilege of showing him around the pavilion.

Table grape growing was another interest; I exhibited at the Sydney Royal Easter Show and received the Commonwealth Certificate of Merit for my grapes. My Muscats were exported to Japan through Sunfresh at the Sydney Markets and shipped via Oriental Lines. I also supplied locally to Gulgong, Rylstone and Mudgee.

One special interest for me has been as Captain of the Lawson Fire Brigade and I have been a member for some 64 years. I started with them in 1949 but couldn't become a member until I turned 16. I am about to be given an award from the Fire Brigade for service.

Community Service with various organisations is close to my heart. You gain so much from mixing with people. I would like to see more people involved with these services. It is good for your heart and soul.

In 2017 I was Australia Day Citizen of the Year recipient.

The Eurunderee School P&C, which I joined at 14, is also special and I am a Trustee and involved in the rebuilding of the historic school. I remember doing a short session with our local radio station 2MG when President of Junior Farmers, and in later years did a half an hour on a Saturday morning, called Bowling Club Sporting Program, always a fun time, often we had guest speakers. Once a fellow won a Minor Singles and

I didn't remember his name, so I called him 'What's his Name' and the club wrote that up on the prize board. Caused a bit of a laugh. 'What's his Name.'

Wise words for my great great grandchildren, honesty always comes to mind. And families must stick together, work as a team. It gives you great satisfaction when you get older and look back on what a good job you have done together. Some sadness comes into everyone's life.

Chapter 17 – Esme Elizabeth Martens

Esme—a trail blazer, a career woman, an independent caring elder of our community and the maker of 1000 exquisite porcelain dolls—an inspiration.

Esme Martens

I was born on 10th March 1939 at Beenleigh, Queensland. My father, Herbert Martens, ran a banana farm, where we lived until I was four. I am the eldest child; my parents were in their thirties when they had me. I have three brothers, two of whom are substantially younger than me.

My father wasn't in the army during the Second World War because he only had sight in one eye. He was seconded into the Civil Construction Corp because he was a qualified builder and sent to work on Somerset Dam. My mother, Elizabeth Schloss, had to close our family home and rent to be near him.

I didn't see much of Dad for a while and would run and hide under the bed when he came home as I didn't know who he was.

After Somerset Dam he was sent to work on the Dry Dock in Brisbane, where we eventually bought the home and it has only recently been sold.

My earliest memory is going to my cousin's wedding when I was four years old. My mother was a dressmaker and had made me a wonderful pink dress. I had pink ribbons in my long hair and black patent leather shoes. I also fondly remember playing Cowboys and Indians with my brother and going fishing and crabbing and swimming in the Brisbane River after church on Sundays and catching yabbies on a dam on our property.

I have done a lot of family history research and my family came here in the 1860's. My father was illegitimate, Father Unknown is written on his birth certificate, although now his name is known. Dad was raised by his grandmother. My mother's family came from Hatton Vale.

I started school at Wynnum West then later went to Wynnum State High School till the Intermediate Certificate, then I caught the train to Brisbane State High School. I won a Commonwealth Scholarship to go to University.

I wanted to become an engineer as my dad was a builder after the war and I used to go with him to building sites. I had a long walk to school and would see men on work sites and building bridges and I thought I would love to build and construct a bridge.

I did a Civil Engineering Degree and then I embarked upon an Economics Degree, first studying at night and then finishing by external study. I don't think I was the brightest student, but I worked hard as I hadn't done many of the subjects needed in the course, e.g. manual drawing. I was the only woman doing the course, and that was for the four years. In 1972 I was fortunate to win a scholarship with the Local Government Engineers Association and completed a Construction Management Certificate from the University of NSW. I also studied and obtained a qualification as a local

Government Engineer and Town Planner. At age 60 I obtained a Diploma in Front Line Management.

I played basketball and was a runner at school, but I am not really into sport, I am more of an academic but have loved craft.

As a child I loved dolls but during the war it was impossible to buy dolls as during the war everything was rationed. My mother persuaded a neighbour to let me have a doll her daughter had outgrown.

Later in life I took up a hobby and made many porcelain dolls. I got involved with this when I saw an advertisement in Bathurst and enjoyed the hobby. I continued the hobby in Sydney and utilised my skills as a dressmaker as I had completed a dressmaking course whilst working at Coraki in Lismore. I have made over 1000 dolls of various sizes and shapes.

After graduation I worked for the Main Roads Department in Queensland. For some time, I was in charge of a road building crew in Central Queensland. Unfortunately, as a woman I was only entitled to ¾ of the male salary and would have lost my job if I married as the Government did not employ married women. I thus moved to NSW where conditions were more favourable and entered Local Government working at Murwillumbah, Lismore, Coraki and Rylstone. At Woodburn Shire at Coraki I became Australia's first female Shire Engineer in 1967.

I have also worked in the disability field for the Office of the Protective Commissioner managing the financial affairs of clients with disabilities and for DADHC as Manager of Engineering Services.

During my working life and later as a Councillor of Mid-Western Regional Council I have achieved a number of milestones including being the first female Shire Engineer in Australia in 1967, the first female Fellow of the Institute of Engineers elected by my peers, nominated as Bicentennial Woman of the Year in 1988, received an AM for Service to Local Government and the community in 1988 and a Lifetime Achievement Award in 2014.

I have been elected to Mid-Western Regional Council four times and am still on Council. I don't belong to any political party. I stand as an Independent and judge all matters on the merits.

My late husband Keith Baxter was the Shire Clerk at Woodburn. I was Shire Engineer there. He had lost his wife when she was quite young. When I was first employed as Shire Engineer there, he told Council they had gone stark raving mad to employ a woman engineer. Years later he asked me to marry him and he became my husband.

Later I had a partner, Bill Costello. When he died, I acquired his land in addition to what I already owned. I run Hereford and Angus cattle on my property at Running Stream. I was from a farming family on my mother's side and Dad has an interest in bananas. As a child I rode horses and tractors on a neighbouring dairy farm. The present drought has made it very difficult for me with little income and huge costs to preserve my breeding stock.

The most important people in my life have been my parents who gave me the opportunities and my husband and then my partner who supported me.

I am proud of my achievements, especially the Evans Head Senior Citizens building, that was built by people who were out of work. A Youth Hall at Coraki again with unskilled labour, the Kandos Sports Ground with voluntary labour each weekend over 2 years. I built bridges in Woodburn Shire and Rylstone Shire. They might not be the Sydney Harbour Bridge, but I am proud of what I have done. I am also very pleased as a Councillor to have seen the Bylong Valley Way sealed and the construction of a new Carwell Creek Bridge, both projects I had supported as Shire Engineer of Rylstone Shire.

I was also involved with many community groups at Rylstone including the inaugural treasurer of Ada Cottage and Chairman of Rylstone Hospital Board for many years. For many years I was Chairman of Kandos Museum having sought its establishment whilst being a member of Rylstone Shire Bicentennial Committee. As a member of the Ilford Running stream CWA Book Committee I researched and wrote several chapters in "Over Cherry Tree Hill". I wrote the chapters on early history of settlement and roads.

I am still a member of Rylstone Historical Society, Cudgegong History Group, many coal Community

Consultative Committees, Crudine wind farm, Mid-Western Seniors Planning Committee as Chairperson.

As far as a memory to hold forever—I have many and cannot nominate just a single event. All are precious to me.

Thank you to the many people who have journeyed with me and helped me along life's way. I have lived here for 43 years and regard it as home. I hope that in some small way I have made it a better place and when I am no longer that I will be remembered by my motto "Actions speak louder than words."

Chapter 18 – Judith Anne Kurtz

Judy, a passionate artist, musician and actress, she paints in her amazing Stony Creek Studio.

Judith Kurtz

Ann without an "E" was what I found on my birth certificate however I have always spelt Anne with an "E".

I was born in Condobolin in a house called Goodwill on 31 May 1942.

My Dad, Henry 'Harry' Pearce, was from Condobolin and Mother, Edith, from Sydney. They met at a dance, possibly at the Trocadero, and married two months later at St Bartholomew's, Broadway, Sydney. It was love at first sight. I have a sister Kay.

My parents were married in an Anglican Church first, but my grandmother made them get married a second time in the Catholic Church. Big thing religion in those days. I was baptised the same day. I can remember my grandmother marching us up to the Catholic school when we went back to Condobolin.

My birth certificate says Dad was a miner. He worked at a mine owned by my grandfather at Tallebung. It was a tin and copper mine where Dad discovered Uranium there when I was 12. Mum was an usherette at a theatre.

School for me began at Hornsby Public then Waitara School. When I was ten, I went to St Joseph's in Condobolin. When I went to scripture lessons at school my friends went to whatever church ran the ones that were more fun, so I went too. I'd gone to Baptist Sunday

School in Sydney. I left school when I was 15. After school I worked in a small corner store, I didn't enjoy it. Then I became a Tracer at the Mid Lachlan Council and was taught on the job. From there at Katoomba Council I was trained at a Draughtsperson, again trained on the job. Alf Munroe was working at the Gulgong Ulan County Council and offered me a job there. I bought a car and travelled back and forth between home at Katoomba and Gulgong. One weekend it snowed so heavily I couldn't get through to go to work.

My first husband and I met at my sister's wedding, he was Best Man and I was Bridesmaid. We had three children, the marriage lasted fifteen years. I moved to Yarrabandai between Parkes and Condobolin where my cousin offered me the jackaroo's cottage. I lived in that cottage for three years. I earnt money painting and taught at TAFE. Art came into my life early I can remember sitting next to a little girl in the playground who was drawing faces. I wondered if I could do it and I found that I could. We didn't have spare paper at home, so I drew around the edges of newspapers and in the Stop Press if it was bare. Faces, horses and dogs were my favourites. I have a drawing of Grandfather I did when I was 13. Dad enrolled me into the Art Training Institute of

Melbourne by correspondence for two years, unfortunately school homework and art together were too much 'those nuns laid it on us', masses of homework. So I didn't finish the art course. I have done other courses and went to TAFE for a year. Oil painting began when I was nineteen. A friend and I went to the Art Society classes at Parramatta when I lived at Blacktown. Every Monday night we attended the different activities. The first time I attended a life drawing class, a young lady was to have posed for us but didn't turn up. A young man offered to pose for us. This was the first time I had ever done any life drawing and was rather embarrassed and tried not to show it. We'd all had a glass of red wine and out came our young man draped in a green chenille bedspread. Each time he changed his pose his private parts were facing me. I thought about whether I was to phase the private parts out or go in really bold with a 6B pencil. So, I went in really bold with my 6B pencil. After several poses he came around to look at everyone's work and said to me, 'Hummmm. Went in a bit heavy there, Dear.'

Fred Martin was a good tonal painting artist of the Max Meldrum method. I learnt so much and owe him a lot. Six students sat at easels and had to paint black and white for three months, then finally we could paint colour. I won Second Prize with a painting of gardenias at Myers Art Exhibition in Blacktown. I won $50. We were very poor and had few clothes and I had holes in my shoes I spent the money on shoes and a cardigan. Fred's classes cost a $1 an hour, so cheap. One person in the Art Society complained about Fred making money and he never taught again. A great loss. I wish I still had some of those paintings I did through his classes. I used to sell a lot of paintings; I entered every competition. A furniture shop displayed some of my paintings for me and as we needed a new bed I arranged for a lay by of a bed and the paintings that were sold, the money came off the cost of the bed.

When my parents lived in Orange my dad made my frames for me and a beautiful easel, which I still use today. Once when he was making some frames and wasn't looking, he cut off some fingers. I was living four hours' drive away and it was raining but I drove to see him at the hospital. My second marriage ended around that time.

In 1988 I attended the Mitchell College Summer School and there I met Ross. My parents had died the year before and that left a big hole in my life. Ross and I were in different classes. People told me that a man had played music on that first night and I had missed it, gone to bed early after the long drive. I didn't miss the second night, I remember him playing in the Common Room, a song called *Eurunderee*, a Henry Lawson poem Ross had put music too. Next day we sat around talking with a group and Ross invited me to watch a tennis match. He was doing watercolours at Summer School and on the last day I asked would he like to go on a painting trip to Hill End with Tony Mason and a group of friends. His eyes lit up and he said yes. He was separated from his wife at the time. There were two bedrooms in the cottage, one for men and one for women. By the end of the week I knew we were meant to be together. I moved to Bathurst and Ross visited. We were married three years later.

Ross built our shed here on the property, a little cottage where we lived for eleven years while he built this house. He was farming and helping other people during those years. Now he's building a shed for his pet tractors, while I paint and sell my works from the studio here.

Diane Simmonds and I published a book, *A Portrait of Mudgee and District*. It has now sold out. Later we did another book for children *Australian Fairy Poems*. I might do another one day. I have painted Mudgee and surrounding areas many times. I love landscapes and still life in oils and pen and pencil drawings, and black and white art. We had a benefit art show here for the Jessop children and it went very well. Ross and I judge at various art shows and do tutorials here in Mudgee and away. I learnt singing from Nancy Featherby and belong to the Stringy Bark Band. My mother in law said early on, 'If you are going to be part of this family you have to join the bush band.' I go to jam sessions with Ross at the Court House Hotel in Mudgee and the Centennial Hotel in Gulgong. Another group I belonged to is the Mudgee Performing Arts Society. Loved that.

A first memory I have is of my Dad in a horse and sulky and me looking up at him.

My parents, Ross, and my three children are the most important people in my life. My parents died together. They were in Intensive Care together and then my sister cared for them for several weeks. Dad died in his sleep and my mother died opening the door to the ambulance. They didn't have to grieve for each other. It was a very sad time for my sister and myself.

Tennis was my sport, although I did play Netball at school and Basketball when I lived in Katoomba.

I now have six grandchildren and I have six great grandchildren, number seven will be born in May. My eldest girl Kerrie lives in Grafton with her husband Mark. My second daughter Donna lives in Caloundra Queensland with her husband Andrew, and youngest daughter Jenniver lives with her husband James in Dallas Texas. I go to visit them every second year and they come here the alternate year.

We enjoy each other's company when our two families get together with Ross's three children, Melody, Alice and Nigel and their families.

Some wise words for my great great grandchildren would be—If they were single, I would say 'choose wisely'. I chose not wisely twice. I am very blessed the third time round.

Chapter 19 – William Warwick Newman

A grazier farmer whose family history goes back to the early days of Mudgee.

William Newman

I was born 12th July 1947 at Braeholme Private Hospital in Mudgee. Everyone calls me Bill, which was a little confusing as my father was also called Bill, even though his name was Victor!

My parents were Victor Neal Newman who grew up at "Nealton", on the Yarrabin Road, Collingwood. My mother was Genevieve Doris Williams from Windeyer. They had seven children and I was the sixth child. I didn't really grow up with my eldest brother and sister as they had gone away to boarding school, so much of my childhood was shared with my sister Louise and my younger brother Roger.

My first memories are living with Mum and Dad at our home at Collingwood called the "Bluff". There were few amenities at the house—no electricity and only 2000 gallons of fresh water. The house was close to "Nealton" where my grandfather and his stepdaughter Eva lived. Eva's house was welcoming, and I recall the lemon syrup she served and the fly papers hanging from the kitchen roof. In later years, Eva would get down her box of family photos and point out who everyone was in the photos. From these photos I gained an interest in my ancestors and through other research I have come to personally know many relatives in Australia and in the UK that I previously had no idea existed.

In 1951, the wool boom meant that my father was able to buy additional land and the family moved to

Malboona, which was further down the Yarrabin Road from Collingwood. I have lived at Malboona since 1951.The property name Malboona, means "bad" and "good" and this depicts our property well, as agriculture is not always easy with good and poor seasons and markets.

Our property was first taken up by William Webb and he built a house of local slate in about 1904, which became our home. It was large and basic with linoleum flooring, Aga stove and outdoor toilet. It was not until 1965 that electricity was put on at the house, replacing a generator. The telephone was a party line which meant that 3 houses shared the same phone line. To make a call, a handle had to be turned to make one long ring for the Erudgere exchange, which closed at 9 PM.

It is strange the things you come across in our house! There is a cellar with makeshift shelves and boxes and I was amazed to find a child's drawing on one of the beams of a head in water with hands up and a label saying "am is drowning" signed by Zadie Webb, who lived at Malboona as a child. Years later, when Zadie was 46, I learnt that she had drowned at Bondi whilst sleepwalking. Was this a childhood premonition?

Dad ran the farm and often camped in a hut up in the back paddock called the "Bluff", built by his father Albert and his brother George. He sometimes went for 10 days at a time. All of us kids helped with the farm work and I learnt how to fence, ride and shoe horses and milk the cow. Back then there was little machinery, so

Dad rode his horse around the paddocks and employed a number of men over the years to help with the farm work. My mother also helped out during shearing by cooking meals for the shearers.

My mother was very strict, but she had a very "laissez fare" approach to what us kids were doing. We had fun roaming the hills, swimming in the creek, as there was water back then and riding horses. When we were to come home, she would blow the car horn.

I didn't start school until I was seven and went to Mudgee Convent. Going to school meant a trip by car or ute from the farm to the corner of Hill End and Yarrabin Roads, where we caught the Windeyer bus. Rex Whittaker was the driver and he drove an old ambulance "bus". The trip along the Yarrabin Road was hazardous as the road was gravel and winding. On one occasion, I fell out of the car on a trip to Malboona from Collingwood and on another occasion my father was driving us in his brand new Holden Ute to the bus and he had a head on collision with a car on the wrong side of the road, at a place which is affectionately called "crash hill" by the family to this day.

After finishing Year 5 and Roger Year 3, we both boarded at All Hallows at Bathurst. I boarded for one year in 6th class and then went on to high school at St Stanislaus College Bathurst until the end of 1963. I then completed years 4th and 5th at St Gregory's College Campbelltown. I was keen on sport and played in the

Stannies under 16's cricket team and the first X1 rugby team at St Gregory's.

After I completed the Leaving, I went to Hawkesbury Ag. College but returned home in my first year to help run the family farm as my father was very ill. I played rugby and cricket on the weekends in local Mudgee teams. My brother Roger also returned home but he was conscripted to the army and spent time in Vietnam. I was lucky, as I was also conscripted but as I was allergic to penicillin, I was rejected.

I have a special memory of Marian, my eldest sister, who died suddenly when she was 40. When I was 14, Marian had left a bottle of red nail polish at home and I painted all my toenails. A few days later, I fell off my horse and was knocked out for a week. I ended up at St Vincent's Hospital, where my sister Marian was training as a nurse. When I woke up 7 days later, I was rather embarrassed to see all my toes painted with the red nail polish!

Our family have always been a farming family, and this began in Australia when my great grandfather, John Newman, arrived in Mudgee in 1857. The John Newman Bridge over McDonald's Creek was named after him in 2018 and there have been 4 generations of the Newman family farming in the Collingwood/Yarrabin area.

My mother's family were from Windeyer and she is a descendant of John Williams and Emma Chick who came to Clark's Creek during the gold rushes in about

1856. Three generations of the Williams family mined at Windeyer including Arthur ("Hat") Williams, my great grandfather and Arthur Walter Williams, my grandfather who died when he was only 48 from dust in his lungs from mining.

I have worked with my brothers throughout my life and we have helped each other in managing our properties. We all shore our sheep at Malboona for many years and until the 1970's mustering was all done on horseback and shearing took about 6 weeks with all the family 'hands on' in the shearing shed. I was the presser and there were no electric presses in those days—all manual labour to press the bales in a manual Koerstz two box press, which was exhausting work! An electric press was later purchased. When motor bikes took over in the 1970's, we were able to muster more quickly, and this reduced our shearing time.

Things have changed over the years and in the 1970's wool prices plummeted, and sheep became known as "land lice" and were worth nothing. This made life very difficult as our farm was best suited to fine wool sheep. We then began grazing cattle as well as sheep, to make ends meet.

Life has not always been easy due to droughts, the present drought being the worst I have known. We have tried to make things more secure to prepare for drought by having a solar pumping system to water our stock, but in April 2018, there was not a blade of grass on the property and as the whole of NSW dried up as well, stock feed became almost unobtainable. This made life difficult at a time when we should be retiring.

In 1973, I met and married Beryl Munt, a school teacher at Mudgee High School who later worked for the Department of Land and Water Conservation. This job took her throughout the Central West and Sydney and left me to batch at home and keep the property going. We have three children Sarah, Mark and Andrew. Two of our children have moved to Sydney, and we now have 3 grandchildren, Otto, Hugo and Akira. My wish for my grandchildren is for them to work hard, care for their family, have tolerance and understanding of others and have happy and fulfilling lives.

We have survived the rough times and still live on the property.

Life has been interesting... You don't realise you are going to grow old until you turn around and you are 72!